SPIR

MILLENNIUM

SPIRITUALITY
for the
MILLENNIUM

SEÁN P. KEALY, CSSp

THE LITURGICAL PRESS
COLLEGEVILLE MINNESOTA

THE LITURGICAL PRESS
St John's Abbey, Collegeville, Minnesota 56321

© Seán Kealy, 1994

Originally published as Spirituality for Today *by the Mercier Press, PO Box 5, 5 French Church Street, Cork, Ireland*

ISBN 0 8146 2369 7

10 9 8 7 6 5 4 3 2 1

Printed in Ireland by Colour Books Ltd.

CONTENTS

PREFACE

SPIRITUALITY IS A popular word today yet one which is all too easily fashioned in one's own image and likeness. It attempts to describe those attitudes, beliefs and practices which animate a person's life especially in relation to the ultimate realities. In the west people are often accused of projecting a privatised, legalistic, self-perfection-seeking individualism in place of an authentic community centred approach emphasising freedom, love and justice. It is so easy to condemn the past and as a recent writer does, accuse Catholics of a Monophysite-flavoured Christology, exaggerated Marian devotions, multiple pious practices, quasi-Pelagian exercises, numerous rules and regulations, comfortable escape-from-the-world retreats, a latent Manichaean dualism and perception of the man–woman relationship, etc.

The following soundings which are obviously incomplete and quite inadequate are part of one person's attempt to work out an authentic spirituality for our unique times at the end of the twentieth century. They are inspired by a firm conviction that the basic Old Testament command is to choose life (Dt. 30:11–20), that Jesus came so that people may have a fuller life (Jn 10:10), that what God is concerned with is not so much whether we are religious or not as whether we are fully alive or not. Yet somewhat paradoxically there is truth in what Chesterton said when he insisted that a man is not a man until he has passed the breaking point and has not broken and that a faith is not a real faith until one has passed through a situation in which all ground of belief has been swept away and yet still, like Job, one insists on believing. Finally there is the conviction that each person has a unique mission in life whether one is fully aware of it in this life or not. As an old statement in the Jewish Talmud once put it 'it is not up to you to finish the work but neither are you free not to take it up'.

Many authors and biblical works and texts have been drawn upon in composing these reflections. However only the major footnotes have been given lest the text become too unwieldy. Several of these reflections have appeared in an earlier form in *Doctrine and Life* and permission to reproduce them is gratefully acknowledged to the editor. Particular thanks are due to Sr Tina Heeran, HRS, who so generously typed most of the originals and to Br Paul Kehoe, CSSp, who put the lot together with his wonderful word-processor.

1

COME, RING OUT OUR JOY TO THE LORD

PSALM 95 IS the Latin *Venite Exultemus*, the psalm which opens the official daily prayer of the people of God. It sets the basic attitude of a Christian life of joy, thanksgiving, worship, remembrance and warning. It is based on the frequent processions of the people towards the Jerusalem Temple, perhaps beginning at the Gihon sanctuary (1 K 1:33), up the Kidron valley and climbing to the Temple mount. Arriving at the Holy of Holies there was a ceremony of adoration and prayer (v. 6f) probably followed by a biblical reading and a sermon – this explains the abrupt transition in verse 7b. The literary style seems clear. First there are two hymns with a call to praise in verses 1f and 6, to be sung by the whole congregation. Then the motivation for praise in verses 3–5 and 7a which was probably sung by a special choir. The ceremony concludes with a prophetic oracle of warning from a temple prophet in verses 7b–11. For the Jew life was a journey to God's rest and the basic attitudes of our daily journey are clearly set out here.

> *Come, ring out our joy to the Lord;*
> *hail the God who saves us.*
> *Let us come before him, giving thanks,*
> *with songs let us hail the Lord.*

There is an old Hebrew saying that what we will have to account for to God in the next life are the things which we could have enjoyed but didn't. I think of the many opportunities for joy missed in my life, the people, the work, the prayer and God. So often my life becomes a life of drudgery like that of the Prodigal Son's elder brother. For there is something radically amiss about a Christian community which is not characterised by a deep sense of hope and joy as it celebrates its Risen Lord. This joy should permeate all our lives and in particular our daily work, even our business deals. Too often Christians present an image of ruthless, cold efficiency in dealing with others, a coldness which permeates even our liturgical celebrations. But one can only invite people to enjoy God, the world, other people, themselves. Nobody, not even God, can make us enjoy. There is a price to be paid for joy. Jesus is the exemplar: 'For the sake of the joy that lay before him, he endured the cross, despising its shame, and has taken his seat at the right hand of the throne of God' (Heb. 12:2).

We Irish, with our sad history and songs, our legends like the Thorn Birds, need to pay particular attention to this basic dimension of the Christian life. Many seem to think that God wants people to be miserable and unhappy. As a character in Brian Friel's play, *Translations*, put it, we are not happy unless we are miserable. Or as John's gospel put it bluntly, people prefer the darkness, to be miserable, to hold on to their fears and anxieties:

> *A mighty God is the Lord,*
> *a great king above all gods.*
> *In his hand are the depths of the earth,*
> *the heights of the mountains are his.*
> *To him belongs the sea, for he made it,*
> *and the dry land shaped by his hands.*

For the psalmist, joy and joyful singing is the proper response when we think of the greatness of the God who is our saviour and whose presence is so evident in the beautiful world around us. Chesterton in a famous verse contrasted the Catholic and Protestant views:

Wherever the Catholic sun doth shine,
There will be laughter and good red wine
At least I've always found it so
Benedicamus Domino.

More than others, we Christians have reason to have joy in our lives because of our belief in Jesus. As John's prologue put it, he is the light shining in the darkness of our world, a light which the darkness has never mastered. It was this belief that enabled Martin Luther to shout out in moments of depression and gloom: 'I have been baptised'.

Come in; let us bow and bend low;
let us kneel before the God who made us
for he is our God and we
the people who belong to his pasture,
the flock that is led by his hand.

For the psalmist, the fact that 'we are his people' and that 'he is our God' is the source of our joy. What do we actually worship? A writer in a recent magazine suggested that, if people admitted what they really worshipped, the banks would have stained glass windows. We can idolise almost anything from wealth to power to sex to nature despite their inability to bring us the deep satisfaction we desire and the inevitable disorders such as anxiety, fear, hatred, anger, inability to trust which result. In his famous little book, *Your God is too Small*, J. B. Phillips described the common distortions of God to be found even among those who claimed to worship the one true Yahweh of the Exodus: God the resident policeman, the parental hangover, the grand old man, the managing director, the puppeteer, the god in a box. A harsh, dry, materialistic and greedy spirit has swept away the political passion and heedless idealism of the 1960s and 1970s according to commentators such as Paul Johnson. The question is whether in this materialistic age we really believe in any spiritual God, the afterlife and the things of the spirit. Is Jesus Christ really the Lord of my life? If so what evidence can I give? What is really important to me? Am I loyal to

Jesus and his Church? The Fathers of the Church often spoke of the sin of 'acedia' or spiritual sloth, a kind of depression or melancholy which is experienced when life is dull and seemingly going nowhere. There is a sense of joylessness when faith no longer issues in hope and gladness – faith and worship become routine. A second symptom is insensitivity to others in need because we are so wrapped in ourselves and not listening to God or others. As Dorothy Sayers puts it 'Sloth is the sin that believes in nothing, cares for nothing, seeks to know nothing, hates nothing, finds purpose in nothing and only remains alive because there is nothing to die for'. The opposite is a Paul who sees a Christian as a soldier in active service or an athlete competing in the games, fighting the good fight, pressing on, stirring up God's gift within.

We are sheep according to the psalmist, using a not very complimentary image for human beings. Recently a farmer told me that there is a lot of money in sheep but they need a lot of minding and a very finely meshed wire fence. Sheep so easily go astray and are unable to extricate themselves. Granted our sheepish qualities which, like members of the AA, we must first admit, the important source of confidence for the psalmist is that Yahweh himself is our shepherd. This image is frequently found in the Bible from the experience of Jacob (Gen. 48:15) to the Exodus (Ps 78:52) to the Exile (Ez. 34:15–16) to the restoration (Mic. 2:12; Jer. 50:19). Yahweh is a compassionate shepherd insists the Old Testament. (Sir. 18:13) who is angry at false shepherds who neglect their duties and run away (Ez. 34:1f; Zech. 11:15–17). Jesus is not surprisingly the true shepherd who lays down his life for his sheep (Mt. 15:24; Lk. 12:32; Jn 10:11; 21:16f; 1 P. 5:2–4; Acts 20:28):

O that today you would listen to his voice!
Harden not your hearts as at Meribah,
as on that day at Massah in the desert
when your fathers put me to the test;

when they tried me, though they saw my work.

For forty years I was wearied of these people
and I said: 'Their hearts are astray,
these people do not know my ways.'
Then I took an oath in my anger:
'Never shall they enter my rest.'

Finally the psalmist goes on to give a threefold warning to his community as he recalls the failures in the days of Moses. Firstly, he insists that we should listen to God today (Dt. 4:40; 5:3; 6:6). All the New Testament authors like Jesus himself were very much present-oriented. The future, and in particular the realm of the possible was left to God. The well-known experience of St Augustine at Milan in August 386 AD comes to mind. Driven mad with pleasure yet desiring to live chastely he flung himself down in tears beneath a fig tree saying 'How long will I go on saying tomorrow?' Suddenly he heard a child's voice repeating the refrain 'Take and Read'. He picked up a Bible and read the first passage his eyes fell on: 'not in revelry and drunkenness, not in debauchery and wantonness, not in strife and jealousy; but put on the Lord Jesus Christ, and as for the flesh, take no thought for its lusts' (Rom. 13:13–14) – almost nine months later Augustine was baptised by Ambrose on Holy Saturday night. He realised the truth of Dante's famous phrase *In la sua voluntade e nostra pace* (In his will is our peace). St Augustine warned his own community not to be like the crow which caws 'cras, cras' (tomorrow, tomorrow). They should be like the dove which gently murmurs 'hodie, hodie', (today, today). Today is in fact the only time we have and now is the time God needs our repentance, our joyful service. If we don't respond today there is an increasing likelihood that we will not respond tomorrow. Business studies suggest if one does not start a new venture in 72 hours then the reality will be never.

In the parable of the arrow Buddha shows how over-speculation on metaphysical questions can hinder liberation.

Buddha describes how a person shot with a poisoned arrow refuses to have the wound attended to until he discovers who shot the arrow, what it is made of, where the materials came from etc. Such a person says Buddha will simply die. Better remove the arrow first and leave all that is not immediately relevant till later.

Secondly, the psalmist warns us not to let our hearts (i.e., our thoughts and decision-making) become hardened, stubborn and insensitive to God's promptings, as happened in the old days at Meribah and at Massah. These were places where the people provoked God's anger and where Moses struck the rock for water (Ex. 17:1–7; Nm. 20:13; Dt. 6:16; 8:15). Meribah (from 'rib' meaning contention or strife) was the scene of Moses' strife with his complaining, bickering and untrusting people. The name Massah (from the verb to 'test'), was given to the region because the people did not trust God's providence and his faithfulness to his promises. The same stubbornness will lead the present generation into exile from the land of rest. Faith in a good God is the basis of true joy. Eric Fromm (*The Heart of Man*) insists that the longer we continue to make the wrong decisions, the more our heart hardens; the more often we make the right decisions, the more our heart softens and comes alive. In O'Casey's *Juno and the Paycock*, the mother faced with the violent death of her son prays: 'Sacred Heart of Jesus, take away our hearts of stone and give us hearts of flesh. Take away this murderin' hate and give us hearts of flesh'. The poet Robert Browning's famous verse expressed the difficulty of being a true Christian: 'How very hard it is to be a Christian'.

In Dante's *Inferno* one is not surprised to find that the lowest level of Hell consists not of fire but of ice and hardness. We find this hardness already in the self-righteous who are so superior and judgmental towards those in prison. Again it manifests itself in our unforgiving attitudes towards others who have sinned against us. It is no mere accident that the Apostles' Creed highlights the forgiveness of sins as

14

the pre-eminent characteristic of the life of the one, Holy, Catholic and Apostolic Church.

Thirdly, the psalmist warns that we must remember the anger of God. God is no marshmallow God. The danger with the sentimental view of God's love is that we take away the passion and the mystery and forget the disturbing and uncomfortable aspects highlighted by the biblical metaphors of the anger of God. The desert generation were excluded from the Promised Land because of their failure to trust in God's guidance. Left to ourselves we are sheep who go astray so easily. But ultimately we can only trust in the goodness of God and God's all-powerful love. This is the true meaning of repentance.

The author of Hebrews gives a very valuable commentary on Psalm 95. For him the Jews did not achieve rest even when led by Joshua (the Old Testament name for the Greek word Jesus). If Joshua had provided rest God would not speak of another day (Heb. 4:7–8). True rest can only be achieved by sharing in the grace of our compassionate Christ who leads us into true rest. Yet paradoxically we need 'to strive to enter into that rest' (Heb. 4:11).

By definition a Christian is a person of hope, a hope based not on an optimistic or pessimistic view of society but on a belief in God's loving compassion seen in Jesus. That is why an Albert Camus could comment 'I shall not try to pass myself off as a Christian because, even though I share the same revulsion from evil, I do not share your hope'. Like many inspired by Friedrich Nietzsche he considered that Christian hope was a cowardly escape from grim reality which should rather be faced with courage. Likewise Nikos Katzanzakis the author of *Zorba the Greek* learned from Nietzsche to distrust every optimistic theory. Only a woman's heart feels the need of consolation. A religion claiming to fulfil human desires is merely a refuge for the timid and unworthy of a true man: 'The faith most devoid of hope seemed to me not the truest perhaps but surely the most valorous'. For Katzanzakis the last temptation to be overcome is the temptation to hope. No wonder he had inscribed on his tomb in Herakleion in Crete 'I hope for nothing. I fear nothing. I am free'.

What would you like inscribed on your tombstone?

2

A PRACTICAL
SPIRITUALITY

IN SEARCH OF Excellence, by T. J. Peters and R. H. Waterman
(Harper & Row, 1982), is an interesting study of success in
business, of how to combine an atmosphere of encourag-
ement to taking initiative with a concern for the common
good. The aim is to see how a company will survive the challenge of the 1980s with its three prime needs of efficiency
around the basics, regular innovation and the avoidance of
calcification. The authors have read widely and draw on a
wide series of studies such as a British researcher's examination of the inertial properties of organisations which showed that 'companies often hold on to flagrantly faulty as-
sumptions about their world for as long as a decade, despite
overwhelming evidence that the world has changed and
they probably should too' (p. 7).

In their research, of what they considered to be excellent
companies, they found that the primary way to understand a
company's orientation is to listen carefully to the way its
members talk about themselves. They were struck by the
dominant use of story, slogan and legend as the members
tried to explain the characteristics of their institutions. However, according to the authors, success depends on a company having a few firm, clear and well understood values to
which, all, at every level of responsibility, are expected to
believe in and live up to.

A key attribute of an excellent company is that it is a
learning company which realises the importance of keeping
things simple despite overwhelming pressures to complicate
things. 'Small is Beautiful' is their effective philosophy and

one-page memos are the ideal. The result is that they are a lot more divided up and a lot less tidy than conventional wisdom seemed to require. Smallness induces manageability and above all commitment. For such companies something besides cost usually came first and that was being particularly close to the customers and being willing to listen and learn from them.

The real role of the chief executive is to manage the values of the organisation. These values are defined more by what executives do than what they say. For leadership fails when it concentrates on sheer survival. Institutional survival properly understood is a matter of maintaining values and a distinctive identity. The latter are not normally transmitted through formal written procedures but by softer means, by stories, myths, legends, metaphors, and the like. Excellent companies are unashamed collectors and tellers of stories, legends and myths in support of their basic beliefs. The annual report is a good indication of a company's shared values. Such a report should make clear what they are proud of and what they value. One interesting conclusion is that success in instilling values had little to do with charismatic personality or personal magnetism. On the contrary it derived from an 'obvious, sincere, sustained personal commitment to the values the leaders sought to implant, coupled with extraordinary persistence in reinforcing those values' (p. 288). Persistence is vital. Once these values, which are often quite simple and practical (e.g., the first point in IBM's philosophy is 'our respect for the individual' and IBM's best ad was 'IBM Means Service') are accepted, they provide the parameters for initiative. At the same time they are the glue which will prevent the company from disintegrating or flying apart. The discipline of a few shared values provides the framework for the required autonomy. It gives people the necessary confidence to experiment, for example, a confidence which stems from stable expectations about what really matters.

The authors agree with the psychologist Ernest Becker who argues that a person is driven by an essential dualism. On the one hand we need to belong, to be a part of a larger unity while on the other hand to have a sense of our unique contribution to stick out, to be both a conforming member of a winning team and to be a star in our own right. This is the meaning of that promise in the Apocalypse to make the one who overcomes a pillar in the temple of my God. Each individual pillar in a Greek Temple was irreplaceable and thus a symbol of the uniqueness and importance of each person. We desperately need meaning in our lives and will sacrifice a lot to an institution which will give us meaning. But simultaneously we need independence, the feeling that we are at least in partial control of our destinies and that our contribution is necessary and unique. The average worker in an excellent company is expected to stand out, to be distinctive, to contribute, to add ideas, to innovate in service to the customer and in producing quality products. To accept mediocrity is to compromise, to refuse to believe that one is part of something important and great.

Excellent companies, according to Peters and Waterman, if they know one thing, know how to manage paradox in an ambiguous world where clear purposes and objectives for organisations are almost impossible to measure. The simple act of paying positive attention to people has a lot to do with productivity but is difficult to measure. The aim is to cultivate a strong sense of personal accountability down the line, the sense that each person is the company. This means treating people as adults, with dignity and respect. But this the writers make clear is not molly-coddling:

> We are talking about tough-minded respect for the individual and willingness to train him, to set reasonable and clear expectations for him, and to grant him practical autonomy to step out and contribute directly to his job (p. 240).

This toughness is born of mutually high expectations and

peer review rather than emanating from table-pounding managers and complicated control systems. It means an obsession about widely sharing information and preventing secrecy. It means a careful and lengthy screening process for all job applicants. Many of the companies studied were known for bringing would-be recruits back seven or eight times for interviews. This had a two-fold benefit. A company could be more certain about those it wanted to hire and a potential recruit could get to know the company and decide whether he or she could really fit in with its philosophy and culture.

In a religious society, which has experienced the ideals, tensions, rapid changes and inevitable frustrations, which are the story of the Church since its reorientation at the Second Vatican Council, it would of course be wrong to take the model of an efficient profit-making business and impose it in Procrustean fashion. According to Peters and Waterman the fact is that the state of theory is in refreshing disarray, a point that could well be made about many religious societies such as ours. However, excellent companies were characterised by a bias for action, for getting on with it. Even though analytical in their approach to decision-making they are not paralysed by that fact. They get quick action because their organisations are fluid and are marked by a refreshing willingness to readily shift resources and to try things out. Big institutions have often forgotten how to learn. They often seem to prefer analysis and debate to trying things out and end up paralysed by fear of failure. There is the widespread problem of paralysis induced by analysis due to a dependence on over-analysis and a narrow form of rationality where planning and talking about things seem to become almost ends in themselves. The simple fact is that people are not very rational and must be treated as they are. Many western people are amazed to learn that most Japanese do not even have a reasonable organisation chart. For example, it is difficult to discover how Honda is organised, it is so flexible and uses so many project teams. The point is that we need to stop overdoing things, planning, aims, etc., on the rational level. A standard question at one business school is 'How many layers do you think it takes to run the Catholic Church?' The answer most came up with is five, laity, priest, bishop, cardinal, pope. The point is that even in such a huge organisation very few layers are required to make it work.

In brief, my contention is that unless there is a solid core of values accepted by the 'middle ground' in any religious society, the society is doomed to extinction. Such a society can tolerate a fair number of members whose views and values are those of a time which has passed away. In fact they can even provide a valuable service, a reminder of our roots, of the caution needed, the questioning always required, before pushing headlong into horizons unknown and untested. Likewise, a society can tolerate or should encourage a certain amount of explorers ('dreamers, heretics, gadflies, mavericks and geniuses') who are willing to try out new ventures, new ideas and who see orthodoxy as the 'slumber of a decided opinion', to quote the phrase of J. S. Mills. In industry it is never the industry leader who makes the big leap but rather small bands of zealots operating outside the mainstream. One important indication of a company's innovative health is the amount of surreptitious experimenting which is going on. What struck Peters and Waterman was the rich support networks provided by excellent companies so that their pioneers could flourish. But as W. B. Yeats put it, 'things fall apart', unless the centre holds.

There is, then, need for a solid centre which is to some extent at home in both the old and the new. Indeed the problem can be recognised as one of the most constant problems of every congregation and every Church down through the ages. The moderate centre provides the counter-balance in the tension between left and right wings which threaten to tear the community apart. According to the Protestant scholar, James D. G. Dunn (*Unity and Diversity in the New*

21

Testament, p. 385), Peter played such a bridge role to hold together the diversity of first century Christianity. Peter contrasted sharply with James and Paul, the two other prominent leading figures in first century Christianity. These were too much identified with their respective 'brands' of Christianity; at least in the views of those at the other ends of the spectrum. Peter's role is seen in the Antioch episode, in Galatians chapter 2. He took care to hold solidly to his Jewish heritage in contrast to Paul. Yet he was open to the demands of developing Christianity in contrast to James. Thus Peter became a figure of the centre holding the extremes together. His concern for mission led him to broaden as Christianity expanded even at the cost of losing his leading role in Jerusalem. He thus became a hopeful symbol of unity for a growing Christianity. People like James and Paul were seemingly too extreme in their lifetime to serve the early Church as the ideal reconciling image. By the 80s and 90s of the first century after Christ, both Antioch (Matthew's Gospel) and Rome (First Epistle of Clement), saw in Peter the symbol of the centre. It was the Christianity according to the centrist Peter, not that of Paul and James, which succeeded in the early Church and became normative for the following centuries.

Practical Spirituality:
Deep down we all know that much more goes into the process of keeping a large organisation vital and responsive than superiors, chapters, founders' ideals, constitutions, policy statements, questionnaires, new plans,strategies, budgets and organisation charts can possibly depict. The basic philosophy of an organisation has far more to do with its achievements than its economic and technical resources, its organisational structure, innovation and timing. The rumour is that it was the ever young Frank Soughley CSSp who once upon a time spelled out in simple terms the basic Holy Ghost philosophy of spirituality. What we expect of a confrère can

be summed up in three questions: Can you live with him?:
Does he do a day's work?: Does he pray well?

Life Together:
Spirituality is a search for quality in life. The glory of God is
living humanity, said St Irenaeus, that is alive with the more
abundant life which Jesus came to bring (Jn 10:10). This life
contrasts with mere existence – the quiet desperation of so
many today, even in religious life. 'Is there life before death?'
became a popular rallying cry in the 1970s as a protest
against the aimlessness and meaninglessness of so much living. St Augustine who is an excellent example of this rest-
lessness opened his *Confession* by insisting that our hearts
can only find their rest in God himself.

The key New Testament theme of togetherness is an excellent criterion of what the reality of a Christian community
was intended to be. Even to pursue the reciprocal pronoun
'one another', ('allelon') is quite instructive. The following
selection from the one hundred uses found in the New
Testament are best read in their original context:

> *Be at peace with one another (Mk 9:50).*
> *The disciples at Emmanus 'were discussing with one another' (Lk.*
> *24:14,17,32).*
> *You look to one another for approval (Jn 5:24).*
> *Stop complaining to each other (Jn 6:43).*
> *You should wash each other's feet (Jn 13:14).*
> *Love one another; just as I have loved you ... my disciples (Jn 13:34).*
> *Friends you are blood brothers. Why are you trying to hurt each*
> *other? (Ac. 7:26).*
> *I want to be among you that we may encourage one another by our*
> *common faith (Rom. 1:12).*
> *As parts of (Christ's body) we belong to each other (Rom. 12:5).*
> *Love each other, as brothers should, and try to outdo each other in*
> *respect (Rom. 12:10).*
> *Have the same attitude towards everyone (each other) ... if possible*
> *live peacefully with everyone ... (Rom. 12:16ff).*
> *We must no longer pass judgement on one another (Rom. 14:13)*
> *Let us pursue the works of peace and build up the common life. Do*
> *not ruin the work of God for the sake of food (Rom. 14:19f).*
> *Be tolerant with one another as Christ ... accept one another (Rom.*
> *15:5ff).*
> *Give advice to one another (Rom. 15:14).*

Greet one another with a holy kiss (Rom. 16:16).
Wait for one another (1 Cor. 11:33).
... that all may be concerned with one another (1 Cor. 12:25).
Serve one another in works of love ... if you go on biting and tearing one another to pieces ... you will destroy one another (Gal. 5:15).
Let us never be boastful, challenging or jealous towards one another (Gal. 5:26).
Carry one another's troubles (Gal. 6:2).
Bear with one another lovingly (Eph. 4:2)
Be friends with one another and kind, forgiving each other (Eph. 4:32).
Give way to one another out of reverence for Christ (Eph. 5:21).
Always consider each other ('the other') to be better than yourself (Ph. 2:3).
Never tell each other lies (Col. 3:9).
May the Lord increase you and make you overflow with love for one another (1 Th. 3:12).
With such thoughts as these you should comfort one another (1 Th. 4:18).
Comfort and upbuild one another ... think what is best for each other and for the community (1 Th. 5:11–15).
Let us be concerned for one another (Heb. 10:24).
Do not slander one another (Jam. 4:11).
Do not make complaints against one another (Jam. 5:9).
Confess your sins to one another and pray for one another (Jam. 5:16).
Let your love for each other be real ('from the heart') (1 P 1:22).
Welcome each other into your homes without grumbling (1 P 4:9).
In your relations with one another clothe yourself in humility (1 P 5:5).
If we walk in the light we are in union with one another (1 Jn 3:23).

There is much fruit for meditation in this list. One of the most important concepts in the whole New Testament lies behind Paul's idea of building one another up (1 Th. 5:11), or edification. The term means to bring to life, to raise up (Jer. 12:14–17; 24:5–7), to gather together in imitation of the activity of Jesus himself, gathering the lost sheep of Israel. Life to the full is the following of, the imitation of Jesus, his understanding of God, his values, his approach to other people. All of these he summed up as 'to serve not to be served'. In this sense Paul could exclaim that for him to live is Christ. This is the ideal we expect a confrère to aim at, to challenge us to imitate. Christ calls disciples into a new family-type of living as a sign of the coming kingdom – a sign of contradiction (Lk. 2:34). The danger is that we just live next to one another and not together, that we drop our ideals and forget what kind of community Jesus intended the people of God to be. The ancient Church saw itself as a contrast society, a people who, despite their failures, took very seriously the task of being a holy people really living as the salt of the earth. No wonder it is often said today that the greatest service which we can render society is to be simply and truly Christian, to be the Church. There are many ministries in our society which we perform to ourselves and to the world. But the most profound ministry, the ministry of ministries, is the ministry of life. We can give bread, health and justice but unless we can give one another a profound reason to live an even deeper meaning to life – of what value are all the others?

A Day's Work:
Religious life is a wonderful gift. But its freedom can be so easily abused. We all need from time to time to examine ourselves and ask if we do a decent day's work. On the other hand there are those who need to take seriously the Bible's stress on liberation from over-work found in the Sabbath commandment. Some biblical texts provide a useful basis for reflection.

> *Learn a lesson from the way wild flowers grow. They do not work or spin (Mt. 6:28).*
> *Come to me all you who labour and are overburdened (Mt. 11:28).*
> *Master we have worked hard all night and have caught nothing (Lk. 5:5).*
> *Jesus tired by the journey sat down at the well (Jn 4:6).*
> *I sent you to reap a harvest you had not worked for (Jn 4:38).*
> *By such hard work you must support the weak (Ac. 20:35).*
> *My greetings to Mary who worked so hard for you (Rom. 16:6,12).*
> *He who plants and he who waters work to the same end. Each will receive his wages in proportion to his work (1 Cor. 3:8).*
> *We work hard for our living with our own hands (1 Cor. 4:12).*
> *Through the grace of God, I have worked harder than all the others (1 Cor. 15:10).*
> *You know that your work is not in vain when it is done in the Lord (1 Cor. 15:58).*

25

I urge you to serve under such people and anyone who co-operates and works with them ... (1 Cor. 16:16).

We show ourselves servants of God ... as people familiar with hard work (2 Cor. 6:5,10,15; 11:23,27).

You make me feel I have wasted my efforts with you (Gal. 4:11).

The one who has been stealing ... should work hard with his hands at honest labour so that he will do something to share with those in need (Eph. 4:28).

You give me cause to boast that I did not run the race in vain or work to no purpose (Phil. 2:16).

... hoping to make every person complete in Christ. For this I work wearily on (Col. 1:29).

We constantly remember your faith in action, your work in love and steadfastness of hope (1 Th. 1:3).

We appeal to you ... to be considerate to those who are working among you (1 Th. 5:12).

Anyone who would not work should not eat (2 Th. 3:10).

This explains why we work and struggle as we do; our hopes are fixed on the living God (1 Tim. 4:10).

The elders, who do well as leaders, deserve to be paid double, especially those whose work is preaching and teaching ... The worker deserves his wages (1 Tim. 5:17).

The hardworking farmer is the one who should have the first share of the crop (2 Tim 2:6).

I know all about you: how hard you work and how much you put up with (Apoc. 2:2).

Happy are those who die ... they can rest forever after their work (Apoc. 14:13).

Particularly instructive with regard to the theme of deeds or work is the conclusion of Matthew's Sermon on the Mount. Matthew tries to steer a middle course between those who are a law unto themselves, the lawless and the wonder-workers who do their own thing. For Matthew it is not sufficient to prophecy, to exorcise demons even to work many miracles in Jesus' name (Mt. 7:22). Such people can be prowling wolves in sheep's clothing and will be condemned: 'I never knew you. Out of my sight you evil-doers' (Mt. 7:23). The wise person will build his life on the commands of Jesus and produce the fruits of love of enemies, forgiveness seventy times seven and especially concern for the weak and erring. The Vatican Council, above all, invited religious to return to the words of Jesus and only secondly to the spirit of the founders. What a Benedict, a Dominic, a Francis, a Poullart des Places, or a Libermann tried to do was not to construct an original gospel or a new spirituality. Each rather tried to interpret the gospel in a prophetic fashion in the concrete situation, the particular problems and the signs of their times. Thus tradition, even the spirit of the founders, can so easily be a form of laziness and a prison. To be faithful to tradition one must continually create new traditions.

Prayer:

The glue which holds a community together, and which gives quality to their apostolic works and community life is found in prayer. Our basic daily structure is the Eucharist, Morning Prayer and Vespers. Luke, when he has described the activity of the Good Samaritan carefully balances his picture in diptych style with the story of Martha and Mary and the Our Father (Lk. 10:25ff). The need for structured prayer times has come across more and more since the Second Vatican Council. In contrast to the rush for personal prayer 'at the times one feels best', it has often been forgotten what a structured prayer life Jesus himself led – regular synagogue and temple attendance, the daily prayer life of a faithful Jew. Jesus and his family, and the apostles after them, are presented in the New Testament as faithful to the Jewish tradition here. Paul in particular insisted on a liturgy and public prayer life so structured that it would edify the community (1 Cor. 14:26). His intention, to quote the German biblical scholar, Gerhard Lohfink (*Jesus and Community*, Paulist Press, 1982, p. 103), was that a maximum amount of meaningful communication would occur in the liturgy. This would be the exemplar of what a Christian's daily life should be. As we saw in our reflection on the reciprocal pronoun 'one another', Paul insisted that the Christians in the liturgy should wait for one another, greet one another, encourage and console one another, admonish and teach one another and above all show care for one another.

The following brief selection of New Testament texts

provides much food for thought:

Love your enemies and pray for those who persecute you (Mt. 5:44).
And when you pray, do not imitate the hypocrites: they love to say their prayers standing up in the synagogues. But when you pray, go to your private room and ... pray to your Father who is in that secret place. Do not babble like the pagans do (Mt. 6:5f).
He went up into the hills by himself to pray (Mt. 14:23).
This kind of devil is cast out only by prayer (Mt. 17:21).
People brought little children to him, to lay his hands on them and say a prayer (Mt. 19:13).
My house will be called a house of prayer; but you are turning it into a robber's den (Mt. 21:13).
Pray that you will not have to escape in winter or on a Sabbath (Mt. 24:20).
Stay here while I go over to pray ... My Father ... your will be done (Mt. 26:36–44).
Everything you ask and pray for, believe, that you have it already, and it will be yours and when you stand in prayer forgive whatever you have against anybody (Mk 11:24f).
Stay awake and pray because you never know when the time will come (Mk 13:33).
Two men went up to the Temple to pray, one a Pharisee, the other a tax collector. The Pharisee stood there and said this prayer to himself (Lk. 18:10f).
All these joined in continuous prayer, together with several women including Mary the mother of Jesus. (Ac. 1:14).
They prayed 'Lord ... show us therefore which of these two you have chosen (Ac. 1:24).
These remained faithful to the breaking of the bread and to the prayers (Ac. 2:42; 3:1; 6:4ff; 8:15; 9:11,40; 10:4,9ff).
The house of Mary the mother of John Mark, where a number of people had assembled and were praying (Ac. 12:5,12; 21:5; 22:17).
I never fail to mention you in my prayers (Rom. 1:10).
When we cannot choose words in order to pray properly, the Spirit himself expresses our plea in a way that could never be put into words (Rom. 8:26).
Do not give up if trials come, and keep on praying (Rom. 12:12).
Surely I should pray not only with the spirit but pray with the mind as well (1 Cor. 7:5; 11:4–13; 14:13ff).
We pray to God that you will do nothing wrong (2 Cor. 13:7–9).
Pray all the time, asking for what you need, praying in the spirit on every possible occasion (Eph. 6:18).
My prayer is that your love for each other may grow more and more both in understanding and wealth of experience (1 Phil: 9:4–6).
Pray for us, especially, asking God to show us opportunities for announcing the message (Col. 1:3–9; 4:2–12; 1 Th. 5:17–25).
There should be prayers offered for everyone – petitions, intercessions and thanksgiving (1 Tim. 2:1,8; 5:5).
I am hoping through your prayers to be restored to you (Ph. v 4, 22).
We are sure that your own conscience is clear ... pray for us (Heb.

13:18f).
If any one of you is in trouble he should pray ... if one of you is sick ...
the prayer of faith will save the sick person (Jam. 5:15ff).
To pray better keep a calm and sober mind (1 P. 3:7; 4:7).
Use your most holy faith as your foundation ... praying in the Holy
Spirit (Jn v 20).
The smoke of the incense went up in the presence of God and with it
the prayers of the saints (Apoc. 5:8; 8:3f).

Discipline:

These three aspects of living together, doing a day's work and prayer, which are obviously closely and essentially inter-connected, form a good description of our basic spirituality of the Christian life. This life lived in imitation of, or following Jesus, can be described as a contrast society, a middle way between the two extremes portrayed in the temptation and transfiguration scenes in the gospels. The temptation scene describes basically the attraction of a worldly approach to our mission, to give into the values and standards, the lifestyle of the world and its search for comfort, prestige and easy success. Jesus came not to be served but to serve, to give his life, to be in the world but not of the world. He set about changing the values and conditions of the world, to transfigure it. Instead of an army he chose twelve somewhat bewildered disciples. Instead of strength he chose the way of foolishness and weakness, the cross. The opposite temptation is that of the disciples who wanted to stay on the mountain of the transfiguration in a small elite community. Jesus resisted this temptation also. He came down the mountain to face the real world and its problems and broken dreams. He identified with many who failed the world's and Judaism's criteria for success: the sick, sinners, women, tax collectors, the poor. Any Christian spirituality worthy of the name should be an inspiration to take up our cross and follow Jesus' example and go to Jerusalem by the narrow way, *The Road Less Travelled,* to quote the title of a bestseller by M. Scott Peck, MD (Simon & Schuster, New York, 1978).

Scott's psychological analysis of love, grace, traditional

values and spiritual growth is based on his day to day clinical work with patients struggling to avoid legitimate suffering or grow to greater levels of maturity. His first section is significantly entitled with a word seldom heard nowadays, Discipline. Scott begins by insisting that one of the greatest truths is that 'life is difficult' and you can make it doubly difficult by running away from it. The only real security lies in relishing life's insecurity. Most do not see this fully. Therefore they tend to moan about their problems, burdens and difficulties as if life were, or should be, normally easy. Laziness is original sin. Life is a series of problems and the tendency to avoid problems and the emotional suffering involved in them, i.e., legitimate suffering is the primary base of all human mental illness. There is no need to fear depressions, anxiety attacks, and bad dreams. They are merely the symptoms of mental illness which serve to notify people that they have taken the wrong path. They are the beginning of its cure. People are thirsting for integrity to integrate religion into the rest of life after Sunday. Scott points out the interesting fact that psychiatric problems occur with remarkable frequency in people shortly after promotion to a position of higher power and responsibility. What we need to teach ourselves is the necessity for suffering and its value, the need to face our problems directly and to accept the pain involved, 'to deny ourselves, take up our cross daily and follow Christ' as Luke's gospel puts it. *In analysing discipline* Scott proposes *four constructive* techniques of suffering: delaying of gratification or the courage to face and get over the painful first (versus 'Play now, pay later'): the acceptance of responsibility ('If you are not part of the solution, then you are part of the problem'): dedication to truth, honesty and openness (a life of continual and stringent self-criticism in a changing world and a realisation that the sources of danger to the world lie more within us than outside): balancing, the essence of which, is the 'giving up' of conditions, desires and attitudes in the course of an evolving lifetime. Some of the latter he lists as follows:

The state of infancy, in which no external demands need
to be responded to:
The fantasy of omnipotence.
The desire for total possession of one's parent(s).
The dependency of childhood.
Distorted images of one's parents.
The omnipotence of adolescence.
The 'freedom' of uncommitment.
The agility of youth.
The sexual attractiveness and/or potency of youth.
The fantasy of immortality.
Authority over one's children.
Various forms of temporal power.
The independence of physical health.
And, ultimately, the self and life itself.

For us the ongoing problem is to balance the three aspects of
our lives, of life with others, doing a day's work, prayer. Our
lives are never static but in a state of growth, of evolution.
The greatest risk we take in life is the risk of growing up, a
leap which many people never take in their lifetime. Growth
always requires courage and involves risk. We need what is
called a will to grow and to keep growing. Ultimately there
is only one impediment, that of laziness. Although outward-
ly adults, and seemingly even successful adults, a majority of
people remain all their lives psychological children who
have never truly separated themselves from their parents
and the power which their parents have over them. Courage
is not the absence of fear but it involves the moving out
against the resistance engendered by fear into the unknown
and into the future. For Scott the motive and the energy for
the necessary discipline is love. Since the essence of love is
work, or the willingness to move against the inertia of laziness, the essence of non-love, is laziness. Reflecting on St Au-

gustine's famous maxim *Dilige et quod vis fac*, which he translates as 'If you are loving and diligent, you may do whatever you want', Scott points out that we like the 'Do what you want' part while the 'Be diligent' gives us indigestion. For we continue to be adolescents believing that the freedom and power of adulthood is our due. Because we have little taste for responsibility and self-discipline we need to have powers above us to blame for our situation. But the call of Christ and his grace is a call to adulthood, to be a parent unto mankind. For with the peace of Christ's grace come agonising responsibilities. This peace which Christ gives is quite different from the peace which the world gives. It is well described in the Christmas sermon which Thomas à Becket delivers in T. S. Eliot's *Murder in the Cathedral*:

> But think for a while on the meaning of the word 'peace'. Does it seem strange to you that the angels should have announced Peace, when ceaselessly the world has been stricken with war and the fear of war? Does it seem to you that the angelic voices were mistaken, and that the promise was a disappointment and a cheat?
> Reflect now, how our Lord himself spoke of peace. He said to his disciples: 'My peace I leave with you, my peace I give unto you'. Did he mean peace as we think of it: the kingdom of England at peace with its neighbours, the barons at peace with the king, the householder counting over his peaceful gains, the swept hearth, his best wine for a friend at the table, his wife singing to the children? These men, his disciples, knew no such things: they went forth to journey afar, to suffer by land and sea, to know torture, imprisonment, disappointment, to suffer death by martyrdom.

This is what Jesus meant by his peace, his fire of love cast on the earth. To love means work and courage, to be willing to move against our inertia of laziness and the natural resistance of our fears.

We all, like Paul, have our favourite description of what love is. Concretely for us love is other people, especially our fellow Spiritans, love is a day's work, love is an atmosphere of prayer. Many speak of life as an ongoing conversion to God, Jesus, to the Church, to the world. I think that we would add conversion to our own congregation and its all too human face and contradictions. The words which the French Jesuit, Henri de Lubac once used in a *Meditation on the Church*, can well be applied to our congregation also:

I am told that she is holy, yet I see her full of sinners. I am told that her mission is to tear man away from his earthly cares, to remind him of his eternal vocation, yet I see her constantly preoccupied with the things of the earth and with time, as if she wished us to live here forever. I am assured that she is universal, as open as divine intelligence and charity, and yet I notice very often that her members, through some sort of necessity, huddle together timidly in small groups — as human beings do everywhere. She is hailed as immutable, alone, stable and above the whirlpools of history, and, then, suddenly under our very eyes she upsets many of the faithful by the suddenness of our renewals.

3

TOWARDS A THEOLOGY
OF SPORT

CONSULTING A NUMBER of theological dictionaries and
manuals recently, I was quite surprised to find that apart
from one in *The New Catholic Encyclopaedia* there was no article giving a theological reflection on sport. On the occasion
of the Montreal Olympics in 1976 a small booklet of pastoral
reflections entitled *A Christian View of Sports* was published
which declared that:

> *The evangelisation of the sports world is in urgent and pressing need
> of theological reflection and an interpretation and an expression of the
> Christian message as it applies to sporting activity ...*

However, little has been achieved. Yet sport occupies an increasingly important part of our lives.[1] We may joke that
boxers live by the gospel principle: 'It is more blessed to give
than to receive'. Occasionally a story about De Valera stop-
ping in a race to help a fellow competitor who had fallen or a
film like *Chariots of Fire*, makes us stop and think. The film
Chariots of Fire told the story of Eric Liddle who was willing
to sacrifice an Olympic gold medal because the 100 metres
event was run on a Sunday. Likewise in 1988 a young athlete
Barrington Williams withdrew from the Long Jump when he
realised that the final was being held on a Sunday. Thus Eric
Liddle in *Chariots of Fire* proclaims:

> *I believe that God made me for a purpose ... But he also made me* fast.
> *And when I run, I feel his pleasure. You were right; it is fun. But that
> isn't all ...*

To a crowd of his fans gathered around after a race he is not afraid to compare his running to the race of faith:

> *I want you to compare faith with running in a race. It's hard, requires concentration of will, energy of soul ... Everyone runs in his or her own way. But where does the power come from to finish the race? From within ... commit yourself to the Lord and he'll see you through to the end.*[2]

Does our Christianity make any difference in the type of games we play and above all in the way we play them?[3] Was Freud far wrong when he insisted that Christians are 'badly christened' and that 'under a thin veneer of Christianity they have remained as their ancestors were' quite barbaric. One thinks of the experiment of the psychologist Jung, who once psychoanalysed a group of Christians and compared his results with a sample of non-Christians. He found that the motivations of both groups were quite similar. Faith had not reached the depths, the spontaneous reaction or natural impulses of Christians. Like other groups Christians were divided by conflicting economic interests, racial prejudice, class selfishness, nationalist feelings, thirst for power, rivalry for prestige, etc. Yet Christianity involves a distinctive view of God, of people, both men and women and how in particular they should be valued and treated, of power, success, failure, priorities, etc.

The reality is as John J. Pilch, a biblical scholar and professor of preventative medicine points out, that one can be an Olympic gold-medal winner yet be unable to get along with one's fellow athletes.[4] On the other hand, Pilch insists that one could be terminally ill, mentally retarded, permanently disabled and still have a high level of wellness. He identifies five key elements in his picture of wellness:

1) Knowing the purpose and meaning of life.
2) Identifying life's authentic, satisfying, fulfilling human joys and pleasures.

3) Accepting responsibility for freedom of self-determination in life.

4) Finding an appropriate source of motivation – spiritual values and/or religious beliefs.

5) Accepting the need for change in life, the need for ongoing 'conversion'.

Historical Reflection:

In was in the more stable and secure societies of China, India, the Near East, Egypt, Crete, Greece and Ireland (whose Tailteann Games are as old as the Greek Games – circa 1000 BC) that the organisation and competition aspects of games began to appear.[5] An interesting example of philosophising on sportsmanship is found in the Chinese Lu Vu from the early Christian Era:

> *A round ball and a square wall*
> *The ball flying across like the moon,*
> *While the teams stand opposed*
> *Captains are appointed and take their places*
> *No allowances are made for relationships.*
> *According to unchanging regulations*
> *There must be no partiality*
> *But there must be determination and coolness*
> *Without the slightest irritation at failings*
> *And if all this is necessary for football*
> *How much more for the business of life?*

But it was the Greeks with their Olympiads dating from 776 BC and their stadia who have had the most influence. Their games, held in honour of their high god Zeus every four years, took place in the context of sacred pilgrimages. The religious dimension was so important that all wars were postponed for the duration and a high level of amateur sportsmanship and fair play maintained. The reward was a simple crown of laurels. Their famous athletes were immortalised in sculpture and paintings and celebrated by poets such as Pindar, whose odes were intended to be sung by a chorus. For Pindar the hero is the straightforward but silent Ajax. He regarded the popular preference for the clever but crafty Ulysses who robbed Ajax of his rights as one of the greatest injustices in history. He blames Homer for his unfairness to Ajax but his main criticism is levelled at the blindness of the public. Had they been able to judge correctly, then the arms of Achilles would have been awarded to Ajax. Pindar seldom describes the actual contests in which the prizes were won. But by means of mythology and by stressing the indispensable assistance of the gods he creates an atmosphere for the moral and religious instruction which he weaves into his poetry. Even philosophers such as Socrates insisted on the obligation of physical fitness. Plato insisted that to be unable to swim was in fact to be uneducated. Aristotle's view was that a healthy body produced a healthy mind thus developing a properly balanced person.

The conquests of Alexander the Great, 356–323 BC helped to spread the Greek ideals throughout his huge empire. It is quite fascinating to see the impact of this culture of Hellenism on the rather backward culture of Judaism, a clash which has often been repeated in history. A good description is found in Chapter 7, 'In the Gymnasium' of James Michener's popular story, *The Source*. While prowess on the field of battle and physical strength were highly regarded, athletics was not a part of ancient Israelite life. The nature of the game of wrestling described in 2 Sam. 2:12–17 with its rather gruesome outcome, is not clear. However, in the clash with Greek culture the attraction for the young Jews of the stadia and public baths was obvious. A Greek gymnasium was built in Jerusalem and Greek games such as wrestling and discus throwing were played. The problem for the Jews was that such activity involved some recognition of the Greek gods who were patrons of their sports. Worse perhaps was the fact that games were performed in the nude – God had made clothes for Adam and Eve. Some were so attracted and ashamed of their own tradition that a form of plastic surgery to become uncircumcised was adapted.[6] The result was that the strict Jews, such as the Pharisee movement to which Jesus was closest, rejected completely 'the foreign games'. In sharp contrast were the followers of the Hellenistic Herods who built race-tracks and stadia and even endowed the Olympic games. The huge arenas for athletic sports discovered by archaeologists both in Jerusalem and Galilee (at Tiberias and Magdala) show that at least some Jews were quite interested in Hellenistic sports. The Christian antagonism to the pagan atmosphere of the Olympics would lead to their abolition in 393 until they were revived by Pierre de Coubertin at Athens in 1896.

While the Greeks emphasised such games as running, wrestling, boxing and throwing the discus and javelin, the Romans favoured competitions which involved danger and bloodshed, even killing. Under the Roman empire the games and festivals were more often dedicated to the emperor than to the gods as among the Greeks. Further, the old Greek ideal of pure competition ('agon') gave way to the Roman taste for entertainment ('ludi'). The Romans introduced chariot and horse races, boxing, bullfights and gladiatorial shows.

The Roman priests normally superintended the games and were paid from the public treasury. Large sums of money were often bet on the outcome. Among the Romans the number of days given to games steadily increased in the early Christian centuries. Juvenal made the famous criticism that all the Romans craved were two things, 'bread and the circus games'.[7] Shakespeare put their problem well when he said:

> If all the years were playing holidays
> To sport would be as tedious as to work.

There were 66 days given to sport during the time of Augustus, 87 in the time of Tiberias, 135 in the time of Marcus Aurelius and 175 in the fourth century. When the Colosseum was dedicated by Titus after the fall of Jerusalem there were

100 consecutive days of shows and holidays. The Colosseum, which could hold up to 87,000 people, was used for scenes in which entire armies fought mock battles, prisoners and slaves could fight to death, wild animals were slaughtered and even naval battles performed in the flooded arena. The public acceptance of Christianity made many such performances more difficult to accept. But only gradually was the impact of Christianity made.

The historian Theoderet tells the interesting story of how the eastern monk, Telemachus put an end to the gladiatorial shows at Rome on 1 January AD 391. He had arrived in Rome, now officially Christian, when the Roman General Stilicho was celebrating his great triumphs over the Goths. No longer were Christians thrown to the lions. But the games continued as those captured in the war were forced to fight and kill one another for the amusement of the people. Telemachus was horrified that men for whom Christ died should be treated in this way. In his hermit's robes he leaped over the barrier and stood between the gladiators. The crowd roared in anger 'Let the games continue' and he was pushed aside only to come between them again. The crowd began to stone him and urged the gladiators to kill him. As he lay dying a hush descended on the crowd as they realised what their killing really was. The young Emperor Honorius abolished the games. As the historian Gibbon remarked, Telemachus' death was more useful than his life.

One Christian who saw that much could be learned from the dedication of athletes was Paul who frequently drew his metaphors from the games. In 1 Cor. 9:24–27; Gal. 2:2; 5:7; Phil. 3:14, he speaks of running the race with a purpose and in 1 Tim. 1:18; 6:12; 2 Tim. 4:7, he mentions fighting the good fight of faith. In advising the Philippian Christians to live life to the full, to strain towards the future, to run for the finishing line, Paul uses a rare word from the athletic contests, a word found only here (Phil. 3:13f) in the New Testament. Meaning 'to stretch full out' Paul imagines the Christian as an Olympic runner with body bent over, hand outstretched, head fixed forward in concentration, eyes fastened on the goal, making a tremendous effort and determined not to quit. It underlies the necessity to strive, to constantly pursue with determination in order to make life's aim – a Christlike character – a reality in one's life. Some scholars suggest that Paul may have actually witnessed some of these games However, a number of recent scholars suggest that his athletic metaphors do not necessarily result from personal observation. Rather, they are drawn from the traditional use of such imagery in Hellenistic Judaism and among the popular Hellenistic philosophers. Every Greek city had a stadium and athletes were well known heroes and highly rewarded in their cities. There were about 300 important athletic contests in Paul's time. It is possible that he attended the Isthmian Games near Corinth in 49 or 51 and perhaps also sold his leather goods and made Christian contacts there.

There is a classic story about the apostle John. One day a well-known philosopher who was about to go hunting happened to meet John. He was amazed to find such a famous person as John playing with a tame partridge and said so. John in answer asked him what he was doing with a bow in his hand for the hunt. 'Do you,' said John, 'always carry it bent fully and taut ready to fire?'

'No indeed,' replied the philosopher, 'because it would soon lose its elasticity and the arrows would fly neither true nor straight nor fast'.

John answered that the human mind was similar in ways to the bow. Unless it is relaxed at times it cannot follow its search for truth properly. Just as the bow always at full stretch will cease to shoot straight so a mind always at full strength will soon cease to be efficient.

Nevertheless it is a disappointment that there is so little appreciation for and direct guidance about sport in the New Testament particularly in the words of Jesus apart from his brief reference to children playing at funerals and weddings

(Lk. 7:32). Quite likely, in the peasant economy of this time there were almost no organised games among the pious Jews to which he was close. There are of course many New Testament passages which while not referring to sport, yet have an important bearing on sports and a Christian's responsibility. These include passages about the all embracing rule, love and judgement of the Risen Christ, passages which show clearly the reality and universality of sin and our prejudices and self-inflicted blindness in our own causes, passages which stress the importance of our brother (and enemy) for whom Christ died, passages concerning the law especially those concerned with the law of love of neighbour.

Nevertheless, the Christian emphasis on spiritual values seems to have devalued the enjoyment of sports. Thus the mediaeval Christian ideal left little room for the organised practice of sport and bodily exercise except in as much as they contributed to 'gentle education'. The spiritual life was mainly focused on the will and the intellect, the spiritual faculties of the soul. The dignity and importance of the body conferred on it by the incarnation was all too often downplayed. The Renaissance with its humanist emphasis on learning promoted the perfection of individuals but never of classes or groups. The result, according to John Huizinga in his study of the development of sport, *Homo Ludens, A Study of the Play Element in Culture,* was a fatal shift towards overseriousness while still being called 'sport' and 'play'.[8]

> *Sport has become profane, 'unholy' in every way; it has no organic connection whatever with the structure of society, least of all when prescribed by the government. The ability of modern social techniques to stage mass demonstrations with the maximum of outward show in the field of athletics does not alter the fact that neither the Olympiads nor the organised sports of American universities nor the loudly trumpeted international contests have, in the smallest degree, raised sport to the level of a culture-creating activity. However important it may be for the players or spectators it remains sterile. The old play-factor has undergone almost complete atrophy (p. 197f).*

In sharp contrast Hugo Rahner points out that the person

who really 'plays' life will constantly hold the two aspects of comedy and tragedy in tension.[9] While life must be seen as joyful because it is secure in the Father it must also have a tragic dimension because freedom always involves danger and to play a game seriously is to believe that the game can be lost. Rahner's *homo ludens* is a grave-merry person with the humour to laugh in the midst of tears and to be aware in the midst of laughter of a sense of insufficiency of limitation.

In particular the moral zeal and extreme intellectuality of the Reformation and Counter-Reformation led to a semi-manichean undervaluing of the body and its activities in games. Few today would agree with the view of John Wesley when he drew up the rules for his famous school at Kingswood near Bristol, that no games whatever were to be allowed and no holiday to be given until a child left school. A child was expected to rise daily at 4a.m. and spend the first hour in reading and meditation. But no games because – 'He who plays when he is a child will play when he is a man'. One has little difficulty in rejecting such a view of a child's education or of religion in general and our God and his requirements in particular.

Despite many attempts to outlaw and diminish sports; they survived and even grew in variety. Sixteenth century Jesuit schools were the first to introduce games of any kind into the European school curriculum. Thus they attempted to convert what had previously been seem as quasi-criminal activities akin to brawling, drunkenness and prostitution into a means of education. In the eighteenth century the English provided the biggest impulse to the modern development of sport. This took place against the background of the Enlightenment and its aim to overcome theological influence and the influence of priests by a long process of education which focused on the things of this world. In the nineteenth century the industrial revolution and the urban movement played a large part. Transport was revolutionised and the privileges of the aristocracy became available to large numbers of people. By 1900 the western world had realised the value of organised sports and recreation as a release from the pressures of urban industrialised living. Previously, work and recreation were not so clearly separated because such activities as walking and horseback riding were the normal means of travel. It was only gradually that the implications of the Sabbath and the Christian Sabbath were realised by Christians despite many attempts to reject the joyful and playful implications of this wonderful gift of God 'for people'.

Some of the best thinking in mediaeval times was done on the virtue of 'Eutrapelia', the virtue of moderation in the use of recreation. The Greek word originally meant ready wit or liveliness. The virtue was originally introduced into the study of morals by Aristotle in his *Nicomachean Ethics* (4.8). Granted that constant work caused weariness of both mind and body and the fact that play and recreation were basic human necessities, the problem was to examine the concerns of right reason as applied to this area of life. This would mean the exclusion of anything morally evil, the importance of self control at all times and of prudent behaviour as regards time, circumstances and social relationships. St Thomas Aquinas considered this virtue as part of the great cardinal virtue of temperance. Eutrapelia as a virtue was a golden mean between the two extremes of excess and defect in the matter of recreation.[10] Excess in dedication to recreation, would involve the neglect of the important matters of life. Defect would involve taking too little recreation, leading to austere moroseness and boorishness in social relationships. However, too little recreation can be worse than too much.

The Need for Evaluation:
With the problems, achievements and tensions of twentieth century society, sports have become a universal and international feature of modern society. Today medical doctors,

lawyers, business people and politicians are finding their activities under moral scrutiny as never before. Critics are beginning to demand evidence of moral responsibility and a willingness to be self-critical, to step back and reflect on their basic needs, values and ideals, the principles which direct their activities and their concrete responses in particular circumstances. What about sports? One must admit that as in the other areas mentioned there is a long way to go if theologians are to speak to the real concrete situation and dilemmas in which people find themselves.

The GAA:

The Irish GAA experience has been a particularly interesting one because the basic unit of both the Catholic Church and the Gaelic Athletic Association is the parish. Liam Ryan points out that because people identified with parish and county teams to such an extent:[11]

> The GAA has been highly influential in healing the many rifts which have threatened to disrupt and fragment families and communities in Ireland through the years. In this task, common membership of the GAA has been a more powerful healing factor than common membership of the Catholic Church. Men who were deeply divided over Parnell, neighbours who had shot at one another in the Civil War, families who had squabbled over grievances great or small, real or imagined, all soon displayed a greater willingness to forgive and forget when gathered round the goal posts than when gathered round the altar.

Further, he points out that by examining our dominant game and the changes which we have made in them we learn more about ourselves, our society and its dominant values than perhaps by examining our religion. He suggests that our GAA games, which remain among the few truly amateur sports anywhere in the world teach us firstly that we are not the leisurely and easygoing people we like to think we are; in fact that we are less so than our British or American neighbours. Secondly, they are not totally team sports because each player is an individual enjoying a unique autonomy. Is

44

not the same true of the Irish people?

The Second Vatican Council:
The Second Vatican Council is the first Ecumenical Council to mention sports but has only one brief reference in the *Pastoral Constitution on the Church in the Modern World* in the section on Cultural Education.

> There are nowadays many opportunities favourable to the development of a universal culture, thanks especially to the boom in book publication and new techniques of cultural and social communication. Shorter working hours are becoming the general rule everywhere and provide greater opportunities for large numbers of people. May this leisure time be properly employed to refresh the spirit and strengthen the health of mind and body – by means of bodily activity and study; of tourism to broaden the mind and enrich people with understanding of others; by means of physical exercise and sport which help to create harmony of feeling even on the level of the community as well as fostering relations between people of all classes, countries and races. Christians, therefore, should co-operate in the cultural framework and collective activity of our times, to humanise them and imbue them with a Christian spirit.[12]

Modern Popes:
Sport is an area in which it seems the twentieth century Popes from Pius X to John Paul II have ploughed a rather lonely theological furrow. All have regarded the basic potential for good in sport as a fundamental part of the nature of men and women. Pius X supported Baron Pierre de Coubertin's attempts to restore the Olympic Games after centuries of absence. Pius XI, himself a mountain climber of note, bluntly attacked in his encyclical letter *On the Christian Education of Youth*, what he termed athleticism.[13] This involves the subordination of everything else to sporting success and the making of sports as the central concern of peoples' lives. One thinks of the popular saying attributed to the famous coach, Vince Lombardi, 'Winning isn't all important, it's the only thing'.

But it is John Paul II who can be said to have elaborated a theology of sports in his many addresses on the subject.

Michael P. Kerrigan has summarised the following major points in the Pope's optimistic and positive reflections on this topic.[14]

1) The positive attitude of the Church towards sports as contributing towards the integral development of the human person.

2) Sports promote self-awareness of one's strengths and weaknesses and self-discipline with the desire to practice and improve according to our ability.

3) Sports foster Community: John Paul lists characteristics which any coach would be delighted to uphold: loyalty, fair-play, generosity, friendship, solidarity, respect and a spirit of co-operation. Recognising an affinity between sports and the Christian faith John Paul asked athletes –

> *Are not these athletic values the deepest aspirations and requirements of the Gospel message?*

4) Wholesome competition is beneficial – somewhat surprisingly, the Pope sees competition (lit. 'seeking together') in a positive light and is quite optimistic about its potential benefits:

> *There is present among athletes a kind of universal brotherhood, a sincere respect for each person and a lively appreciation for one another's' abilities and gifts. Athletes engage in stiff competition; they like to be challenged and enjoy the excitement of a great contest. But rather than leading to rivalry and dissension such competition, when carried out in a climate of friendship, leads to a still greater mutual respect and fraternal esteem.*
> *A sense of respect for the competitor must never be lacking even in the rightful effort to achieve victory.*

5) Sports are a training ground for life in the world: Thus utilising one's talents, self-discipline, dealing with adversity, learning to work with others, mutually respecting another's abilities, all can help one become a better person, an exemplary citizen and Christian adult. Good sports, according to the Pope, have important goals outside the actual com-

petitions themselves. They –

> *contribute to the construction of an orderly, peaceful and hard-working society and foster friendly relations on an international level.*

6) Sports promote World Peace. They are a propitious element to overcome multiple barriers and strengthen the unity of the human family beyond all differences of race, culture, politics or religion.

7) The Bible, particularly the Pauline letters, offer the basis for theological reflection on the value of sports. Pope John Paul himself frequently turns to St Paul in his own reflections.

Moral Aspects of Sport:

It is generally recognised that sports are worthy of cultivation because they can contribute to the development of different virtues.

Courage: Sports train a person to struggle, to overcome difficulties rather than to give up easily in face of the pains and adversities of life. Thus in an interesting article, entitled *A Sport for Everybody*, Bob Kreigel suggests that through skiing, rock climbing and white water rafting, we can learn how to face and even overcome our fears and anxieties.[15] Through running, swimming or biking long distances we develop endurance and will and learn how to cope with boredom. Through golf we can practice intense concentration and subtle control.

Co-operation: The contribution of team sports is obvious here.

Temperance: Sports can teach a sense of self-control, discipline and order.

Justice: Here there is a specifically Christian contribution by the emphasis on playing the game, being fair to others, having a sense of obligation to the group and respect even to one's 'enemies'.

Humility: Sports should teach one to appraise in a realistic and objective way one's talents and abilities. Perhaps the best contribution is the ability to cope with failure which is the inevitable lot of all. In a world where so many demand instant and constant happiness and success Christians too often try to portray the perfectly successful image and thus fail to reach the many who are struggling to cope with failure and meaninglessness in life. According to a modern study in leadership, *A Passion for Excellence* some of the most renowned 'tough bosses' in business are the most vociferous advocates of 'failure-as-normal'.[16] To fail, learn and try again is seen as normal. They recommend a regular 'this is what we learned from mistakes' bulletin for each new product or project group. Certainly how we cope with failure in sport is an excellent mirror of our struggles in life. We know only too well that the star talent, good tactics and even team spirit cannot guarantee success. There is also needed that ineffable something which can neither be bought or traded which can crudely be described as luck but which if we are honest escapes our calculations and often our merits.

Conclusion:

Sports then are as Christian as the love of God and of neighbour as ourselves which inspires them. They can make us proud, arrogant and superior or can help us conquer our fears and false self-sufficiencies to reach out to others in love and in appreciation of the goodness of God's elegant creation. Sports can be both prayerful and ethically instructive as far too few modern theologians help us to realise. In an interesting issue of *The New Catholic World* (July/August, 1986), John Carmody remarks that –

> *Just as we can thank God for the light of our eyes and the air we breathe, as the Dutch Canon used to pray, so we can thank God for the exercise that helps us see the world more sharply and breathe the air more deeply. The river I see in the middle of a work-out is better focused than the river I contemplate over drinks ...*

The harsh reality is that so often sport in many places has become a monster out of control in a culture so serious and win oriented that its function as a replenishment of the inner spirit and a model for the Christian life is often forgotten. One must admit with many coaches that it is quite difficult to combine a competitive sports philosophy which sees winning as everything with a Christian morality which insists that all is grace, that the first shall be last and the last first and that God, if on any side seems to have a preferential option not for the winners but the losers in life. One must admit the real danger of sports becoming a religion for the many, e.g., the religious terminology often used of faith, spirit, ritual, dedicated, sacrifice, ultimate commitment, stars, also the colourful banners and signs, fanatical supporters and mini-skirted vestal virgins. There is, as Andrew Greeley pointed out, a powerful religious component in many public sports spectacles. This derives from the deep human need to turn a game into a dramatic imitation (Greek 'mimesis') of the war in heaven between the forces of good and evil. We enjoy the drama when we can identify with one side or the other and invest the struggle between the good guys and the bad with a cosmic dimension. Was Eisenhower far wrong when he defined an atheist as a person who watches a Notre Dame–SMU football game and doesn't care who wins?

Perhaps it is an exaggeration, but as some recent writers have pointed out, worship is the most suitable term to describe the behaviour of many spectators. The adoration bestowed on players tends to convince them of semi-divine status. Therefore they often behave like the capricious deities of old and when a referee dares to correct them they get away with a display of petulance, anger and even contempt for lawful authority. Yet what a sorry sight many are when invited to speak on a serious topic on radio or television. Carrying banners and shouting slogans their fans, well named, even attribute miraculous powers to their heroes (e.g., 'Joe Bloggs walks on water'). They chant their names and sing hymns even using such religious melodies as *Adeste Fideles*. Photographs of players and teams are like icons in prominent places in homes. There are sacred writings too which displace the Bible, manuals of instruction, periodicals and annuals recounting the mighty deeds in hyperbolic language. There are 'theologians' analysing the games on radio, television and in the press ad nauseam. One could continue and speak of the financial rackets which dominate many modern games. These are concentrated in the hands of comparatively small groups whose motivation is not play but the acquisition of profits at any cost. Professional Boxing, in particular, comes in for much justified criticism today. Any sport which encourages the will to inflict real injury on an opponent is, to say the least, morally questionable.

It is easy to be negative. One modern writer compared professional football to a powerful drug. He quoted Karl Marx's words inscribed on Lenin's tomb, 'Religion is the opium of the people', drugging them so effectively that they are not conscious of their miseries. He goes on to add that today as Marx would add other names of the narcotics which are corrupting western society he would not fail to include professional football. I wonder what Marx and Freud would make of a statement in *Time Magazine* about the recent Olympic Games of which it was a sponsor:

> If an allegorical hero is to be found in the Games, it is Youth in general. A time of life is held still. For two weeks nothing ages; at least that is the illusion. The Olympics make the illusion grand. All the world agrees with it.

Yet many I suspect would agree fully with George Orwell's comment on British sport that it has nothing to do with fair play: 'It is bound up with hatred, jealousy, boastfulness, disregard for all rules and sadistic pleasure in witnessing violence: in other words it is war minus the shooting'.

Certainly many people in the past have misinterpreted

the value and even the necessity of myth and illusion. Psychologists such as Carl Jung have helped rehabilitate myths and enable us to see the vital contribution which they can make to our coping with the tension between an ideal future or past and an all too imperfect present. For such myths represent an imaginative reaching out, an attempt to portray the deeper things which lie beyond empirical observation and simple deduction or scientific description and provide insight into the answers of God himself. Just as the therapeutic situation enables the patient experience the past as present so the myth enables the believing community experience the future as present. Somewhat surprisingly the novelist Thomas Mann pointed out that while in the life of the human race the mythical is the early and primitive stage, in the life of the individual it is a late and mature one.

Writing, in *Caritas Magazine* 1989, on 'Sport and the Mentally Handicapped', Dr Alex Turnbull suggests that the motto 'Sport for all' speaks volumes and can be applied to old and young, black or white, male or female, thin or fat, mentally normal or retarded. Sport allows our humanity to be expressed in a physical form and can be a universal communication, healing divisions or creating them also. Using the acronym SPRINT its benefits can be listed as socialisation, physical relaxation, incentive, new boundaries and team-work.

Thus there are many positive aspects to modern sport as we have seen. In his study on aggression, Anthony Storr sees competitive sport as a healthy ritualised expression of aggression which can make violence and war less likely. A good comparison can be made between football and theatre with its Aristotelian effect of 'catharsis' or purification. The field is the stage and the players are the actors with their histrionic antics, dances of triumph, embraces of joy and victory. A psychologist could see a sports event as a kind of drama with the beneficial effect of purifying the emotions of the spectators and players. But is this always the case? If it is to be so, sports need the cutting edge of a Christian dimension. On the other hand Christianity, can be said, to need sports. For they are an example of signs of transcendence in action. As Irenaeus put it long ago, the glory of God is a person fully alive.

4

A TRUE PROPHET

ONE OF THE most important and difficult problems in the story of religion is the problem of distinguishing whether a person is a true prophet or not. By what authority did a Mohammed or a Marx prophecy? Prophecy seems to have been an ambiguous phenomenon in Israel from its first appearance. The ecstatic prophets could easily be accused of madness or sickness (2 K. 9:11; Hos. 9:7; Jer. 29:26). They were accused of venality (Mic. 3:5–12) and of leading the people astray (Hos. 4:5; 9:7–9).

But the problem is not only a political or economic one. It pervades such modern movements as renewal in the Church, liberation theology, the charismatic movement. It shows one's ideas of God, the Church and in particular authority in the Church. What are the criteria which one uses to distinguish the voice of the true prophet from the false prophet? Is it possible to have objective and verifiable criteria? Many attempts have been made to distinguish such criteria. Thus Joachim Wach *(Types of Religious Experience, Chicago, 1965)* in a pioneering study of the history of religions lists four basic criteria in an effort to distinguish genuine from bogus religious experience, to ward off psychosis attempting to substitute for religion. According to Wach a valid religious experience involves ultimacy, totality, intensity and community. It is a response, not a passive experience of ultimate reality and does not end up in the worship of the trivial. It involves the total person and not just the mind, will or emotions – it does not remove the necessity of thinking critically, choosing wisely and experiencing widely. It involves a confrontation with the matter of life and death, meaning and purpose and is at least occasionally intense. Genuine religious experience can never be a mere isolated privatised experience, nor an excuse for selfishness. It has a missionary thrust reaching out beyond oneself to others and to community – even monks struggle to keep alive a compassionate sense of the wider world.

The criterion of Gamaliel is familiar (Ac. 5:34ff) – if the undertaking is of men it will fail but if it is of God it cannot be stopped! Gamaliel quoted two examples of unsuccessful movements from the explosive political situation of the times. The first one, perhaps inserted anachronistically, concerned a Theudas who led a band of people up to the Jordan with the promise that they would walk dry-shod across a divided Jordan like the Exodus of old. The second example was the Galilean Judas, who started a revolution against the Romans on the principle that tax was due to God alone. However, this criterion of success or failure is a criterion of patience and hindsight. It is of little real value in a concrete situation where one is confronted with a difficult choice of following or not a person who claims to be a prophet. Time and time again the prophets were rejected by their contemporaries and recognition and veneration only came after their deaths, e.g., Jeremiah who consistently prophesied Judah's doom yet it only took place some forty years later; John and Jesus have yet to be accepted by many Jews. Further it would lead to such simple conclusions, e.g., Mohammed was a success, therefore he was a true prophet as he claimed. The problem obviously is not as simple as all that. What is one to do with the myriad of voices which clamour for attention today? Is there no further criterion? The criterion of success at most can be described as a negative criterion. Can one say that failure is certainly due to the absence of the power of God, but not all successes can be attributed to God? Yet Christianity is no easy success story. It is about the most certain fact of crucifixion and is essentially paradoxical, a triumph of failure. According to Joseph Blenkinsopp (*A History of Prophecy in Israel*, SPCK, London 1984, p. 46) despite the Deuteronomic criterion of falsification it seems that an unfulfilled prediction (e.g., Amos 7:11; Mic. 3:12) did not necessarily result in a loss of prophetic credentials.

There is also the problem where biblical texts seem to contradict one another. Thus Is 2:4 and Mic. 5:3 speak of beating swords into ploughshares while Joel 4:10 reverses the ploughshares into swords. Compare Ps 68:19 and Eph. 4:8; Mic. 5:1 and Mt. 2:6; Hos. 11:1 and Mt. 2:5; Hos. 13:14 and 1 Cor. 15:54–55. At one time dreams seem acceptable if judged by the Mosaic tradition (Gen. 15:12; 37:5; 40:4–8; Num. 12:6–8; 22:1ff). Yet Jeremiah (29:8f) can warn against those who dream dreams. Obviously the will of Yahweh had a different pastoral thrust for different times and circumstances.

What is a Prophet?

A popular view of Old Testament prophets which is reflected in the *Book of Sirach*, rabbinic Judaism and in Qumran and also clearly in the New Testament (Acts 3:24; 1 P. 1:10ff) is that they were people supernaturally equipped by God to predict the future. However the modern critical consensus according to Brevard S. Childs (*Old Testament Theology in a Canonical Context*, SCM, London, p. 122) agrees rather on the following four central features:

a) 'The Old Testament prophets were "men of insight", although limited by their time-conditioned horizons, who spoke to the people of their day regarding the issues of the day'

b) The secondary or later material added over a lengthy period by disciples to the original sayings of the prophets was 'used to broaden the original limited focus of the prophets by updating the first oracles for another historical period'

c) 'The prophets stood in a long history of tradition on which they were dependent'. The original prophets were primarily proclaimers rather than authors – *forth*tellers not fore-tellers – who couched their oracles in traditional, stereotyped speech forms

d) The phenomenon of Old Testament prophecy is not unique to Israel but reflects many similarities of like nature from the world of comparative religion.

The most frequent word to describe prophetic utterance in the New Testament is 'fore-tell' (Lk. 24:27, etc.), but as John L. McKenzie writes (*Dictionary of the Bible*, p. 698) it is a common misconception of Old Testament prophecy that it means prediction. This idea cannot be based on the common formula 'that it might be fulfilled' as in such cases as Mt. 2:15, there is obviously no prediction, rather

> there is reference to an Old Testament character or event which illustrates the reality of the process of salvation, the reality which is fulfilled in Jesus Christ.

Modern scholars see the function of a prophet as not merely to predict or announce the future. Rather it is to interpret the situation of the time in the light of the traditional teaching, the covenant, and to pronounce judgement on the contemporary situation in the name of God. The prophet is best understood as a traditionalist who has little or no *new* knowledge which his contemporaries did not have. The material of their communications is not to be seen as the result of telephonic communications from Yahweh. Basically it is the common knowledge of the people derived from the Mosaic tradition and applied to contemporary events with the 'envelope' of such conventional phrases as – 'Thus says Yahweh' and the literary forms such as oracles. Their message was primarily directed to and to be understood by their contemporaries. In Vawter's phrase they spoke to the conscience of the people and were the 'troublers of Israel' like Elijah was to Ahab.

Thus we can appreciate Congar's definition of a prophet as

the man who does not allow the means to become an end, the outward forms to be pursued and served for their own sake; the man who constantly reminds us that the real truth of the present lies further and at a higher level than the present and who fiercely points to the spirit that lies behind every shape of letter (Quoted in Concilium, *Vol. 37, p. 1).*

To the prophet idolatry is the basic sin and as in the Deuteronomical history it is followed by punishment. Yet repentance and true faith brings salvation from the covenant God in whom alone security and prosperity lie.

In this way modern study has brought the prophets 'down from the clouds' as it were. While not denying their divine inspiration we can appreciate their humanity and their struggles with the people of their time. Their people in turn had a problem like us today of distinguishing true from false prophets.

False Prophets in the Old Testament:

In the Old Testament there were two balancing institutions of kings and prophets. A prophet was very different from a king. Like the Pope, whom Stalin dismissed, he did not have any army or external power. His strength, which was spiritual, lay in the free response of the conscience. He was a witness to the transcendent, to values which were rooted in the covenant. But the prophet and his vision of reality as God saw it, was vital in Jewish society. It was due to such men and their vision and interpretation of events that the small Jewish nation survived such dreadful disasters as the Babylonian captivity. In sharp contrast so many of the smaller nations of the ancient world sooner or later lost their identity in the melting-pot of the great empires.

Although Abraham was the first person in the Old Testament to be called a prophet (Gn. 20:7; Ps 104:15) yet *the* prophet, the norm for all subsequent prophets to come including Jesus himself, was Moses and his covenant (Dt. 18:15–19). Hosea seems to have been the first person to describe Moses as a prophet (Hos. 12:13). Some seven features of Moses can be seen as typical of a true prophet:

1. A personal call into God's presence from Yahweh himself (Ex. 3:1ff) – the false prophet takes the office on himself (Jer. 14:14; 23:21).

2. The prophetic interpretation of the purpose of history and current events as Moses interpreted the Exodus events (Is. 45:20–22).

3. An ethical and social concern (Ex. 2:11ff; Dt. 24:18–22).

4. An involvement in public affairs including a criticism of the king. Moses demythologised Pharaoh and showed that all human authority has limits in its claims.

5. A combination of both proclamation, judgement and also prediction (Dt. 18:15ff).

6. The use of symbols (Ex. 17:8; Num. 21:8; Jer. 19:1ff; Ez. 4:1ff).

7. Moses was an intercessor, a man of prayer, standing in the breach between the people and God (Ex. 17:19; 22:30ff; Num. 27:5; Dt. 9:18; Jer. 7:16; 11:14; 1 K. 13:6; 2 K. 19:4).

Anybody in the Old Testament could be a prophet; Eliseus was a farmer; Amos a shepherd; Isaiah a nobleman; Jeremiah and Ezekiel priests; Miriam, Deborah and Hulda were women.

Not surprisingly, the problem of distinguishing true from false prophets was no less acute in the Old Testament than it is today. False prophets have been differently described as ecstatics, professionals, cult figures, pro-establishment propagandists or even super-patriots. A recent proposal is that the missing element in false prophecy is the classical prophets' affirmation of Yahweh as creator of all peoples and a consequent participation in the canonical monotheising process.

In the time of Elijah (1 K. 18) there seems to have been a clear cut distinction between the prophets of Baal and the prophets of Yahweh. But by the seventh century with both using the same language 'Thus says Yahweh' and appealing to the same authority there seems to have been a major crisis in distinguishing between the two. According to J. Crenshaw (*The Interpreters Dictionary of the Bible*, Supplementary Volume, p. 702) the struggle produced criteria for distinguishing bogus from authentic ones.

> One set of criteria concentrated on the quality of the message: does it come true? (Deuteronomy); does it offer false hope? (Jeremiah); was it mediated through dreams or visions (Jeremiah); is it given in service of Yahweh rather than Baal (Deuteronomy). Another set focused on the prophet: has he stood in the divine council? (Jeremiah); has he been called by God? (Jeremiah); does he behave in an exemplary fashion? (Jeremiah). In time a different sort of criterion arose: did the prophet live during the period from Moses to Ezra?

Crenshaw concludes that the post-exilic Judaism found prophecy sorely deficient and that it turned to apocalyptism and wisdom for spiritual guidance. Childs disagrees and insists that the formation of the Old Testament Canon set up a scriptural norm for distinguishing the true from the false prophet.

When Jeremiah confronted Hananiah, carrying his yoke symbolising servitude, a yoke which Hananiah broke, thus giving the opposite message of freedom, how could the people distinguish true from false? Could Jeremiah have been certain that Hananiah was a false prophet a term introduced by the Greek translation into the text at this point. Only later when given a new saying to deliver to Hananiah did Jeremiah realise that Hananiah had not uttered a true oracle (Jer. 28:12–14). How could King Achab choose between the contradicting messages of Micaiah and Zedekiah (1 K. 22; Jer. 4:10, etc.). No less than three times the Old Testament discusses the criteria by which true and false prophets can be distinguished, i.e., Dt. 13 and 18; Jer. 23 and Ez. 12–14.

Deuteronomy: The Deuteronomic history was written to explain the disasters which had overwhelmed the two kingdoms as the result of their failure to listen to the criticisms and warnings of the prophets. The *Book of Deuteronomy* faces the problem of the craving of people to unlock the secrets of the future and to know the purposes of God in critical situations. It clearly rejects (Dt. 18) all forms of magic and necromancy as incompatible with the loyalty due from God's people. 'The truth embodied in these prohibitions,' writes Cunliffe-Jones (*Jeremiah*, Torch Series, p. 112) 'is that no true way to God involves attempting to escape the moral transformation which his word works in us. Attempts to find a neutral non-moral road inevitably lead to a weakening of moral character.'

The way for Israel is the way of divinely appointed prophets, a succession of men like Moses, the normative prophet, whom God will raise up to guide Israel. The aim of the Deuteronomist in raising the question 'How may we know the word which Yahweh has not spoken?' even when it has been spoken in his name, is to protect the community. Evidently false prophets were frightening the community with warnings of impending disaster – it is the opposite situation for Jeremiah. Chapter 12:1–5 proposed the criterion of correspondence with the established claims of Yahweh faith. Chapter 18 gives a negative test which is exemplified in Jeremiah's exchange with Hananiah (Jer. 28:9). Obviously it is a *short* term prediction which is the test here given but at best it is a partial test as a false prediction is often fulfilled also. Chapter 13 gives a further test of prophecy, a theological test. Here signs and wonders are ruled out as they may be merely a test of Yahweh. The test of the false prophet is whether he leads after other gods or is he faithful to the revelation of the God of the Exodus, i.e., the teaching of Moses.

Jeremiah: It is to be expected that Jeremiah who lets us into his mind as no other prophet does, should show us his search for practical criteria to identify the false prophets with whom he was so often in conflict. For Jeremiah false prophecy is rebellion punishable by death (Jer. 28:16f). Jeremiah's critique of false prophets is threefold, firstly their character and mission, secondly, their kind of message, thirdly, the form of their message. Firstly, Jeremiah denounces the false prophets as men of immoral conduct themselves (23:14 adultery and lies) who make no effort to turn the people from evil doings. These false prophets are self appointed (*v* 32) and not sent by Yahweh and have no access to the 'sôd' or council of Yahweh. The call of the prophet was the basic experience in his life which changed his career. These call scenes are among the most impressive parts in the Bible from that of Moses at the burning bush to Isaiah in the temple. A true prophet was convinced by this experience that he was set apart by Yahweh to mediate his word to his people, to turn them back following Yahweh with all their heart.

Secondly, the content of the false prophets' message corresponds to their character. It was basically a flattering popular message. Like the institutional prophets they were always tempted to prophecy a message of 'Peace, peace' when there was no real peace with God or among themselves – it was a peace without regard to the moral conduct of the people which is basic to true shalom in its proper sense. Thus in reality they are liars. The true prophet is a prophet of judgement on sin, of repentance, as critical of false optimism as he is of false pessimism. Jeremiah offers a blunt moral test of a prophet:

> *Among Samaria's prophets*
> *I saw unseemly deeds;*
> *They prophesied by Baal*
> *and led my people Israel astray.*
> *But among Jerusalem's prophets*
> *I saw deeds still more shocking;*
> *Adultery, living in lies,*
> *siding with the wicked,*
> *so that no one turns from evil;*
> *To me they are all like Sodom,*
> *it citizens like Gomorrah (23:13f).*

That God bluntly rejects such prophets:

61

> *I did not send these prophets,*
> *yet they ran;*
> *I did not speak to them,*
> *yet they prophesied.*
> *Had they stood in my council,*
> *and did they but proclaim to my people my words,*
> *They would have brought them back from evil ways*
> *and from their wicked deeds (23:21f).*

Finally Jeremiah condemns these prophets for their misuse of the traditional forms of prophecy – their claim to have a divine origin for their dreams and visions when in reality they were lies and their words were stolen from one another. The real thing says Jeremiah is as different as straw from wheat, the word of God is like a consuming fire or like a hammer which breaks a rock and can be recognised by its effects on people and events.

Jeremiah, as Childs points out (p. 139), does not deny that God is free to change his mind:

> *he does not say to Hananiah: 'God spoke through me of destruction, and therefore he cannot say something different through you'. Instead he allows for the possibility that God has a different purpose. However, he then sets up a criterion for determining the truth of Hananiah's claim. God has in the past always spoken of judgement. If he now changes his plan, he will demonstrate it in history. If God then reveals the truth of Hananiah's prophecy of imminent salvation by his action, Jeremiah is fully prepared to acquiesce. In sum, the issue at stake is theocentric: what is God's purpose? It is not psychological: how does Jeremiah know whether or not he is right?*

Exechiel: The answer of Ezechiel (Chs 12:21–14:11) is basically that of Jeremiah. They have not been sent by Yahweh but prophesy out of their own minds, a shallow message of optimism, of peace where there is no peace, with a similar indifference to the moral behaviour of the people. The real word of Yahweh is always a summons to repentance.

In the final article of his interesting study entitled *Confrontations with the Prophets* (Fortress Press, Philadelphia, 1983) H. W. Wolff discusses how we recognise false prophets. He suggests the following distinguishing marks of the true prophet: points to deserved judgements, normally making things much more difficult and not easier for his audience; is characterised by a lack of self-confidence in his own difficult work. In contrast with the false prophets portrayed in Micah and Jeremiah who seek the favour of their listeners the true prophet can depend only on his own discernment of God's will and his belief that the word he speaks really comes from God (a charismatic criterion). A further characteristic is the ethical criterion which stresses honesty and integrity in public judgements. Inviting his readers to imagine an eight foot by eight foot cube of nuclear explosive hovering over the head of every single person, Wolff remarks that true prophets today will not hide such realities of today, even less 'the vast tissue of guilt, mistrust, fear, profit-seeking and hostility which led to and are still leading to, these stores for the annihilation of mankind' (p. 74).

New Testament: In a sense the New Testament adds little to the criteria which we have seen in the Old Testament. For the newness of the New Testament is above all the person of Jesus in whose life, teaching and activity were so closely united. Thus Jesus himself is the New Testament's criterion. One can easily see in him the many aspects of a Jewish prophet from his call, his interpretation of Jewish history, his ethical and social concern, his involvement in Jewish affairs, his proclamations and predictions, his use of symbols, his intercession, his failure. He regarded himself as a prophet (Mk 6:4; Lk. 13:33).

According to J. D. G. Dunn *(NTS* 1977–78, pp. 175–198) Paul's treatment of the problem of false prophecy is the most valuable and perceptive within the Bible as a whole.

For Paul, prophecy was very important (1 Cor. 11:4f; 12:10f; 14:5) among the spiritual gifts.

> *Make love your aim and earnestly desire spiritual gifts, especially that you may prophesy (1 Cor. 14:1).*

Prophets as builders of the Church were next to apostles in Paul's churches (1 Cor. 12:28; 14:3ff; Eph. 4:11). But like the classical prophets, Paul had reservations about ecstatic speech discouraging the use of glossolalia in communal worship and stressing the importance of rational speech which was understood by the congregation. Not every word of a prophet was to be taken as God's word but was subject to safeguards and controls (1 Cor. 14:32). Paul asks of prophets whether they really confess Jesus as Lord and serve the good of the community, his body (1 Cor. 12:1ff). The sign that one has crucified the flesh with its passions and desires is that one has the fruits of the spirit which are love, joy, peace, patient endurance, kindness, generosity, faith, mildness, chastity (Gal. 4:22f;). The edification of the community was the test for Paul (1 Cor. 14:4,31; 1 Jn 3:11–18; 4:7–21). Thus in brief Paul has three criteria or tests, the test of recognised revelation (1 Cor. 12:1ff), of community benefits (1 Cor. 14:1ff) and above all of love in contrast to the impatient rudeness of many charismatics (1 Cor. 13:1ff). I. H. Jones (*The Contemporary Cross*, Epworth Press, 1977, p. 57f) sums up the difficult decisions which Paul is asking the Corinthians to make:

> We ought not to underestimate what Paul is asking of the Corinthians. He is asking them to make the kind of decision we find so difficult – for or against public lotteries, for or against comprehensive education, decisions which are complicated by prevailing trends and attitudes. He is asking them to make the sort of decision the ancient Israelites had to make when they witnessed the battle between Hananiah and Jeremiah, to decide between two prophets both acting in character and one of whom must be disastrously wrong if only they could see which it was and what a wrong decision might mean. That was the kind of decision which Paul was asking of them. Like those who listened to Jeremiah, those who listened to Paul in Corinth had to take up a challenge to realistic responsibility for one another.
>
> Like those who watched Jeremiah, those who had watched Paul had little to go on except that this man took his suffering for God seriously and responsibly and had no doubt that this was what faith was about. But there was a further element in the total context in which their decision had to be made. Paul was addressing the community to whom it could be said by way of conclusion: 'the grace of the Lord Jesus Christ and the love of God and fellowship in the Holy Spirit, be with you all' (13:13).

According to John, redemption and judgement have been brought through a crucified Messiah. Timothy Gorringe (*Redeeming Time*, Darton, Longman and Todd, London, 1986, p. 106) comments that John is 'in debate with a humiliated and defeated people who are not cowed by their defeat but still dreaming of a kingdom which will end the domination of Rome'. John insists that the Messiah has already come and that his kingdom is not of this world. It is based on 'a refusal of the power of this world, of coercion and techniques of persuasion, moral and physical brute force'. The new age of the Spirit, the advocate of the crucified Lord, the comforter and counsellor of the community, has dawned. As in Paul's view the Spirit makes possible the confession that the crucified Jesus is the Messiah come in the flesh (1 Jn 4:2; 1 Cor. 12:3). John's second criterion is that only he who loves is born of God and knows God (1 Jn 4:7; Jn 3:7; 17:23ff). Both for Paul and John the Spirit of the crucified Jesus creates a new kind of community with new values.

For Matthew to say 'Lord', 'Lord' and to prophesy in Jesus' name it is not sufficient to enter the Father's kingdom (Mt. 7:22f). Even working miracles and exorcisms is not a sufficient sign that the person is not an evil-doer (Mt. 7:23). Good deeds and in particular, hearing and putting into practice the words of Jesus is the only way to build on rock and to be wise (Mt. 7:24ff). Self-criticism is an essential quality of every Christian who is paradoxically called to be wise as the snake but yet simple as a dove. Thus for Matthew a higher level of obedience to the law of love, forgiveness and compassion is the answer to false prophecy (Mt. 7:15–23). Luke attempts to present a picture of the early Church like Jesus himself empowered by the Spirit and living a community life of good news to the poor. Essentially it is untroubled and unhindered by obstacles and factions and is still in fundamental continuity with Israel and Jerusalem.

While the New Testament can speak of certain individuals as prophets within the Christian community (Mt. 10:41) on the other hand in the New Testament every Christian is a prophet in society at least potentially. Peter made this clear at Pentecost in the words of Joel:

> Spirit upon all flesh ... visions ... dreams ... and they will prophesy (Ac. 2).

They certainly had problems with prophets in the early Church as 1 Cor. bears witness and the problem of criteria arose. Far from naive acceptance, Paul recommends submission of one's message to the judgement of the community and the tradition which he handed on.

The early Christian, not surprisingly, tried to provide rules to guard against abuse as the famous passage in the Didache, *The Teaching of the Twelve Apostles*, shows (par. 11:3–12):

> Concerning the Apostles and Prophets, act thus according to the ordinance of the gospel. Let every apostle who comes to you be received as the Lord but let him not stay more than one day, or if need be a second as well; but if he stays three days he is a false prophet. And when an apostle goes forth, let him accept nothing but bread till he reaches his night's lodging; but if he asks for money he is a false prophet. Not everyone who speaks in a spirit is a prophet, except he has the behaviour of the Lord. From his behaviour, then, the false prophet and the true prophet shall be known. And no prophet who orders a meal in a spirit shall eat of it; otherwise he is a false prophet ... but whoever shall say in a spirit: 'Give me money or something else, you shall not listen to him, but if he tells you to give for the benefit of others in want, let none judge him'.

The problem of the attractiveness of false prophets had always existed in the Church and is of particular importance today when the Spirit is breathing anew in the post Vatican period. One's answer will always depend on faith and the acceptance of the cross. Perhaps there will always be difficulty in distinguishing the voice of the true prophet, but an important way to establish criteria is to reread the Biblical discussions of the problem and apply them to our situation. The Church has always had difficulties with prophetic spirits down through the centuries especially as the Church became more organised and thinks that it has come of age. There is no need for prophets if the Church and especially its leaders are what they should be. A prophet who does not come from the organisation and whose thoughts disturb because they do not derive from the popular teaching of the day will always be a problem to us. A prophet will always be somewhat of a surprise as no order, rank, experience, sex or even age can be excluded *a priori*. It was the singing of a child which led the dilatory Augustine to repentance. The story goes that Ambrose was elected bishop because a child cried out 'Ambrose is Bishop'. The correct attitude to evaluation by a Christian was well summed up by Paul to the Thessalonians:

> *Do not stifle the Spirit and do not despise prophetic utterances but test everything and keep what is good in them and avoid the bad of whatever kind (1 Th. 5:19–22).*

As one writer put it only because the early Christians took account of the ecstatic and the non rational and the enthusiastic did it recognise the need for checks and balances. Too much rationality can be as harmful as too much non-rationality (J. D. G. Dunn, *ET*, October 1982, p. 13).

5

THE SIGNS OF THE TIMES

CHRISTIANITY IS PARADOXICALLY a triumph of failure. It is a tension of high expectations and the carrying of the cross. Therefore, it is not surprising that one frequently hears about 'a failure of nerve' in carrying out the mission of Jesus. In fact concern for mission is an excellent thermometer for the state of Christianity. Recent years have witnessed a considerable amount of pessimism with quite a number of missionaries, to use Thoreau's phrase, 'living in quiet desperation'. We all tend to have our pet evidence and pet solutions as we view the world in Procrustean fashion. We select the evidence to explain what is happening and offer the solution that suits our personal prejudices – the vocation crisis, the number of dedicated missionaries who are leaving or 'defecting to the west' as it is called, the bishops, who unfortunately, as it is put, live up to our expectations. Many were struck by Cardinal Suenens' unanswered question at a recent Synod as to why the young are attracted to the gospel and yet reject the institutional Church.

The missionary movement was at least superficially and often popularly associated with the colonial experience. Today colonialism is a dirty word and, though most missionaries have successfully made the transition to a new era, many are exhausted and confused by the new situation and the new values. The new ideas and directions of the Second Vatican Council, especially on cultural relativity and ecumenism, cannot be understood and adapted properly overnight. In a sense only the superficial can change easily. The modern phenomenon of rapidation with its consequent 'future shock', has left many missionaries unsure how to cope. Not least of all, there is the problem of recognising past failures, accepting cultural relativism, the rejection of the 'going to hell' syndrome, while keeping up missionary enthusiasm.

One could attempt a psychological analysis of the current pessimism. Many reasons can be suggested. Some stress a person's endocrine system, because in fact many attitudes are simply due to a person's physical condition. Others emphasise perhaps the inner dissatisfaction which can so easily be projected on to others, particularly those in authority; the secret unbelief and the desire to have the best of both worlds, like the lady who wanted the shoe big on the inside but small on the outside; past failures and sinfulness and what Paul called his 'sting of the flesh'; the reluctance to believe that grace is sufficient for us (2 Cor. 12:7); especially that fundamental constituent of the human condition, fear, that exhaustion and feeling of hopelessness, that lack of confidence in one's society, its philosophy and future which frequently in history seems to overtake people of a high degree of material prosperity and lead it to self destruction.

In coping with the tremendous mystery of evil and the variety of suffering in the world, it is difficult to steer a course between believing in the total corruption and the total goodness of people. Today we are haunted as never before by desires for an impossible perfection, especially from leaders of Church and State, not to mention ourselves. The media bombard us with superficial hopes for instant solutions and blind us to the need of a prolonged struggle with ourselves and our problems if anything of value is to be achieved.

Yet what Christian would deny that the Spirit is at work in Eastern Europe in recent years, shaking us out of the comfortable ruts into which we so easily settle, challenging our feelings of being so terribly alone, insisting that God is alive, although some suggested that he was dead, that he is in control of history and working in our lives, yet a God whose thoughts are evidently not always our thoughts?

The example of Eusebius, the 'Father of Church History', is a salutary warning in any attempt to read the signs of the times. It warns of the need for extreme caution in identifying the kingdom of God with any political system no matter how favourable it is to Christianity. After Constantine's victory at the Milvian Bridge in 312, Eusebius became one of the chief spokesmen for the new vision of a Christian world empire. In fact he became an agent for Constantine to whom he had personal access. He believed that the Pax Romana which had begun under Augustus was the expected kingdom of peace foretold by the prophets.[17] He saw in Constantine and his descendants 'the saints of the most High' of Daniel's vision.[18] These he thought, would rule Rome, the fourth kingdom, until the end of the world when it would be destroyed and the final judgement would come.[19] In more modern times the signs of the kingdom have been seen in such phenomena as colonialism, de-colonialism, secularism, capitalism and socialism, feminism, the option for the poor.

The Christian response to a critical situation is neither a pessimistic nor an optimistic one. Probably never in history has the situation looked so good for people and at the same time so bad as today. A pessimist, who looks at the half-empty part of the glass, will point to wars, hunger, poor leadership, population explosion, economic inflation, chaos, terrorists, ecological problems – 82 major conflicts around the world since 1989 with more than 9 million refugees. An optimist will describe the great progress which people have made, the growing concern for people, for justice and the rights of the working person, the technological progress which can eliminate misery and poverty. But the Christian who faces the mystery of suffering, is neither pessimistic nor optimistic according to the data. He is hopeful, based on a faith in a good God, whose love he has witnessed in the life of Jesus. This is the hope which kept a Paul and a Bonhoeffer going when all seemed lost.

But what precisely is this God up to in our world today?

A Christian believes that God is working out the salvation of humanity despite our perversity. God is the missioner and our duty is to co-operate with him as far as we can. But the question is not only what is he doing, but what is he saying to our world today? In brief, what are the signs of the times? What are the events, situations, movements which reveal to us what God is asking of us today. This approach takes the present seriously and attempts to build on the premise that God continues to be available to people through their present experience. If there is an on-going communication from God to man and woman, an on-going summons from God to contemporary people, what can we discover about it from our historical situation and from human aspirations today?

The expression 'signs of the times' is a typically popular expression whose meaning everybody understands until asked to define it precisely. It is well known that the committees at the Second Vatican Council, who prepared the document on *The Church in the Modern World*, experienced serious problems in trying to interpret the signs of the times. They finally settled only for the most general signs such as change, transformation and progress. The famous 1968 Medellin Conference of the Latin American Bishops was more daring and declared that the signs in Latin America are found especially in the social order.[20]

The contribution of Pope John XXIII is a good place to begin a reflection on the 'signs of the times' as it was he who gave the biblical term its current popularity. When he convoked the Vatican Council on 25 December 1961, he spoke of our duty to be vigilant, to keep our sense of responsibility awake because

distrustful souls see only darkness burdening the face of the earth.

He spoke of our need to reaffirm all our confidence in Jesus who has not abandoned the world which he redeemed, but is always with us even to the consummation of the world.[21]

In particular Pope John suggested that we should make our own the recommendation of Jesus that one should know how to distinguish 'the signs of the times', a reference to Mt. 16:1–4; Lk. 12:54–56. These texts are an attack on the hypocrisy of many like the Pharisees, Scribes and Sadducees, the pious people of Jesus' Day, with whom he seemed to have the most difficulty. Not to recognise the signs of the times is hypocrisy.

Such a type of religion is the self-assured piety which actually separates from God, a self-righteous blindness which blinded and deafened people to God's activity, to the good news of his loving reconciliation. Religion so easily degenerates into a frozen thought world, a closed system. Thus many of the professional religious of Jesus' day actually failed to see God's activity before their very eyes, in their midst. They refused to co-operate with what he wanted to do although they claimed to be completely dedicated to God and to his will. They missed Jesus standing in their midst. Jesus was as obvious a sign of God at work in the world, as Matthew's red sky in the morning is a sign of a storm or Luke's south wind and cloud, rising in the west, are signs of heat or rain. In Luke the passage on the weather signs is the fourth in a series of five parables (the Waiting Servants, the Sleeping Householder, the Man in Charge, the Way to Court), in which Jesus foresees the coming political crisis and invites his fellow Jews to read the signs of the times and act accordingly. In the final parable (Lk. 12:57ff), the insolvent debtor on the way to Judgement is Israel. Israel is in a critical situation. She must choose either to join with God's way embodied in Jesus or refuse and pursue the path of zealotry and nationalism and collide with the Roman power and end in destruction. Clearly, the signs are not learned puzzles which only the few clever ones can solve, but are as it were, staring people in the face if only they will repent and ask to see.

There will always be such blind people even like

Caiaphas or Pilate, who think they are acting for the good of the people. A Cyrus of old (Is. 45:4–7) thought that he was in control of history while all the time it is God who is at work reconciling the world to himself (2 Cor. 5:19).

Jesus is the exemplar sign of God in the world. However, as Simeon put it, Jesus is a sign to be contradicted because he is set for the rise and fall of many (Lk. 2:34). Simeon foresaw that the coming of Jesus would compel people to take sides and to reveal their deepest and innermost selves – a dominant theme in John's Gospel.[22] Simeon alludes to Isaiah's sign given to the house of David (Is. 7:14), a section of Isaiah which includes the stumbling-stone reference.[23] There is also an allusion to the 'waters of contradiction', the place where Israel was unfaithful to Yahweh.[24]

Therefore, it cannot be expected that at any time in history, Jesus the sign, is popularly or completely accepted. On the contrary, his signs have been a continual source of contradiction and rebellion even to this day. In fact one of the true tests of a prophet of old was that he spoke an unpopular doctrine. While the Church, according to the Second Vatican Council always has the duty of scrutinising the signs of the times and interpreting them in the light of the gospel, they need to be carefully distinguished from the spirit of the age which all too often casts its spell on Christians who are so easily blinded to their insidiousness.[25] The naturalistic and this-worldly atheism of modern secularity, although undermining the very basis of Christianity, actually proved attractive to a number of theologians in the mid-1960s. More recently the Marxist 'praxis' has exercised quite an attraction despite Marx's own statement that religion was alien to his theories, which he believed to be incompatible with Christianity. Nevertheless, Liberation theologians claim to find many of Marx's insights quite valuable in confronting the problems of the modern world. For he was deeply affected by human suffering and concerned to improve the human lot. He criticised the philosophers for only interpreting the world while for him the real point is to change it. The Church had all too often been content to condemn social evils while making little real effort to abolish them. The tendency was to concentrate on the individual and to hope for the eventual transformation of society. But to see in Marxism 'the signs of the times' is often a naive interpretation. Marx's ideal was a life not unlike that of an English eighteenth century country squire, working in the morning, hunting in the afternoon and reading in the evening. He believed in the dignity of the human person as essentially a creative being. Like killing a cow for its hide and throwing away the rest was the reduction of a person to one mechanical function such as hacking at a coal face or turning a screw thousands of times a day. Marx rightly argued that every institution or society tends to create a philosophy of life, a set of values or a doctrinal system which protects the centres of power in society and makes it easier for those in power to rule. Even religious ideals can be a subtle way of protecting those in privileged positions in a privileged institution.

Praxis, for Marx, is a revolutionary approach aiming at transforming the real world and real society, to make it more human. Like much liberation theology however, it is based on the somewhat naive assumption that Capitalism alone is the great oppressing system in the world today and that Marxism or Socialism, despite their, at least equally depressing record, can achieve peace, freedom and general prosperity. One thinks of the basic truth expressed in one of G.K. Chesterton's Father Brown stories:

> 'I'm afraid I'm a practical man,' said the doctor with a gruff humour, 'and I don't bother much about religion and philosophy.'
> 'You'll never be a practical man till you do,' said Father Brown.

To condemn the Pharisees and Zealots of yesterday and today is not difficult. However, it is not so easy to be positive and to search out the signs of today's times and to describe them. Pope John claimed to see in the midst of so much

74

darkness and prophets of doom:

a few indications which augur well for the Church and humanity.

He suggested that useful teachings could be learned from so many bitter experiences as the bloody wars of our times, the spiritual ruins caused by many ideologies. The questions, which scientific progress has raised, have obliged people to become thoughtful, more conscious of their own limitations, desirous of peace and attentive to the importance of spiritual values. For scientific progress has accelerated that progress of closer collaboration and of mutual integration towards which, even though in the midst of a thousand uncertainties, the human family seems to be moving. This for Pope John facilitated the apostolate of the Church. The result is that many people who had not realised the importance of its mission in the past are, taught by experience, today more exposed to welcome its warnings.

The Church is 'no lifeless spectator' but has followed:

step by step the evolution of peoples, of scientific progress, and social revolution.

It has:

opposed decisively the materialistic ideologies which deny faith

and has witnessed the rise and growth of the immense energies of the apostolate of prayer, of action in all fields, a clergy better equipped in learning and virtue for its mission, a laity more conscious of its responsibilities and duty to collaborate with the hierarchy, to which he adds the immense suffering of entire Christian communities, which we might not easily recognise as a sign of the times. Therefore, although the world may appear profoundly changed, he saw also the Christian community as in great part transformed and renewed, strengthened socially in unity, reinvigorated intellectually, interiorly purified and thus ready for trial.[26]

The Second Vatican Council and the Signs of the Times:
The Second Vatican Council, therefore, took up this theme of the signs of the times and treated it expressly in six documents – in 1963 on Liturgy, in 1964 on Ecumenism, in 1965 on the Apostolate of the Laity, on Religious Freedom, Life of Priests, The Church in the Modern World.[27] A reflection on this theme in the Vatican Documents is a useful guide for the interpretation of the signs of today.

On Liturgy, the summit towards which the activity of the Church is directed and the fountain from which its power flows, the Council described as a sign of the providential dispositions of God in our time and as a movement of the Holy Spirit in his Church –

zeal for the promotion and restoration of the Sacred Liturgy.

This restoration can be seen from the emphasis on Scripture, the use of popular languages and adaptation to different cultures. Here we have the recognition of the fifty-year-old liturgical movement which had gone through many dark nights before it was recognised as God's activity.

On Ecumenism, the Council exhorted the Catholic faithful to recognise the signs of the times and to take an active and intelligent part in the many efforts being made in prayer, word and action, to attain that fullness of unity which Jesus Christ desires – knowledge of one's own belief and of the beliefs of others is pronounced a prerequisite of all true ecumenical work.

On the Apostolate of the Laity the Council notes the ever growing and inescapable sense of solidarity of all peoples. Stressing the rights and duties of the laity to apostolic activity on their own account and in their own sphere it sees the task of the lay apostolate:

to take pains in developing this sense and transforming it into a

On the Life of Priests, the Council emphasised both the priest's appropriate and responsible independence from the bishop and their necessary collaboration with the laity, e.g., recognising *along with them* the signs of the times, uniting their efforts with those of the laity and conducting themselves after the example of Jesus who came not to be served but to serve. Priests should be sincere in their appreciation and have an unfailing respect for their just liberty, dignity and special role, be willing to listen to lay people, give brotherly consideration to their wishes and recognise their experience in the different fields of human activity.

In the Council's final document, *The Church in the Modern World*, as it turned its attention to the problems of the modern world (e.g., marriage, morality, culture, economics, the population issue, the international community, war and peace), the Council took a new approach, in contrast to its other documents. This new approach began, not with abstract theory, but with a survey of the real-life situation of people in today's world, as modern catechesis is inclined to do. Actually this was the only major document which resulted from a suggestion made (by Cardinal Suenens) during the actual discussions of the Second Vatican Council. The document sees the duty of the Church always as –

> scrutinising the signs of the times and of interpreting them in the light of the gospel,

of responding to the questions of man, to his joys, hopes, griefs and anxieties especially of those who are poor or afflicted, in a language intelligible to each question. The Council sees the great characteristic of today's man as 'profound and rapid change', bringing serious difficulties and imbalances, e.g., abundance of wealth, resources and economic power, yet a huge proportion tormented by hunger and poverty, illiteracy. Never was man so keenly aware of freedom, yet new forms of social and psychological slavery appear. There is a vivid sense of unity and dependence, yet of political, social, economic and racial camps and conflicts. People painstakingly search for a better world without working with equal zeal for the betterment of their own spirit.

> The people of God believes that it is led by the Spirit of the Lord who fills the whole world. Moved by that faith it tries to discern in the events, the needs and the longings which it shares with other men of our time, what may be genuine signs of the presence or of the purpose of God. For faith throws a new light on all things and makes known the full ideal which God has set for man thus guiding the mind towards solutions that are fully human.[28]

Each Person's Search:
The treatment of the signs of the times in the documents of the Second Vatican Council was not complete. The following examples are also quite useful in dealing with this difficult theme. Pope Paul's reflection in his speech which inaugurated the fourth session is worth mentioning.[29] Studying the signs of the times, he tried to adapt

> the ways and methods of the sacred apostolate to the growing needs of our times and the changed conditions of society.

Thus he announced the creation of a new permanent structure in the government of the Church: 'The Synod of Bishops'.[30] The apostolic exhortation *Evangelii Nuntiandi* insists that the signs have different meanings in different contexts and countries.[31]

The search for signs of God's activity is not confined to any one group in the Church, where all are called to be prophetic. The task of discerning the signs of the times is a never-ending one and rarely results in clear cut statements that are universally valid. A reading of the parables in Matthew 24–25 shows the need for cautious vigilance. Each person should examine his own situation and community, make a personal list and become involved. For each sign can be taken as a question addressed to oneself.[32] Two lists have come to my attention in recent years and are proposed here as examples for reflection. The first is by Max Warren who was General Secretary of the Church Missionary Society for some twenty-one years and is found in his book *I Believe in the Great Commission*.[33] In a chapter entitled 'The Recovery of Nerve', he sees the following seven positive signs in a time of so many 'negative, world-denying signs', as a help to recover our faith that God, the uncontrollable, is in control of history. They are encouraging factors which provide the setting and new challenges and opportunities for the Church to exercise her missionary task today.

1. The Compassionate Society: Despite the violence and suffering, a compassionate society exists, the like of which the world has not seen before.[34] Television brings disasters before our eyes even as they are happening and calls forth compassionate aid from so many societies and governments all over the world.

2. The Passion for Justice: On a world-wide scale, to a degree never known before, people protest against discrimination, against political, social and economic injustice. Whereas some forms of Marxism, such as Stalinism, are clearly deviations to be resisted, its most modern ideal was a fiery protest against the horrors of the nineteenth century industrial society.

3. The Search for Meaning: Science, philosophy and religion are all radically pressing the question: What is man? The young, who are amazingly united across the world, personalise the issue, asking: Who am I? without being content with the answers of the older generation.

4. Interiorisation: Possibly, the most important sign is the hearing of 'the still voice' of 1 Kings 19:12. This is a protest against the pressures of our mass society, a refusal to be content with its offering of 'bread and circuses', a hunger for the eternal and the enduring, a form of prayer, not unlike the fourth and fifth century 'flight to the desert'.

5. *The Search for Belonging:* Among the numbers of uprooted, primitive cultures, among urbanised peasants, among the traditional Christian Churches, whose members have often voted with their feet, people are seeking a spiritual home where they can feel that they can belong, e.g., the fast growing Pentecostal Churches, the Independent Churches and in particular the Charismatic movement, which is bringing a freshness of faith to many for whom institutional religion had little appeal.

6. *The Search for Unity:* There is a universal move toward unity which finds expression, for example in the impressive international community of scientists, so that from now on, because 'we will either be destroyed together or survive in a new community', our future is singular, not just different stories of different peoples.[35]

7. *The Ecumenical Movement:* This is a spirit long before it achieves any institutional form. It is the answer to Jesus' high priestly prayer of John, chapter 17, and is an example of the Spirit articulating our longings.[36]

Our second list of what he calls four points of growth in Catholic religious life or 'four areas of thought and behaviour which are increasingly important to many people', comes from Cardinal Basil Hume's impressions of the Catholic Church in Western Europe and in America after the 1977 Synod on Catechetics.[37] Despite the abundant wisdom, skill and experience and the astounding scientific and technological achievements of modern man, many sense a malaise. For people are trapped by secularism which finds the ultimate explanation of everything including man within the restricted limits of what the senses and the human mind can discover and measure, and the values of the consumer society which promises beatitude in the multiplicity and variety of its products. People suffer from the double reaction of apathy and violence.

Cardinal Hume's four growth points, which he sees at

least as seed and promise for the future and a challenge for the united Christian conscience, are:

a) Prayer – despite the apparent rejection of the institutional Church there is a movement of prayer in parishes, convents, monasteries, family groups, which transcend denominational barriers and inspire us to live as Christians.

b) A Consciousness of the social dimension of the Gospel which should inspire Christians to work for a better and more just society.

c) A Growing Awareness of the importance of the dignity of the human person.

d) A Universal Tendency towards the development of caring and believing communities. The impersonal character of urban industrialised society has given rise to a desire for small, face-to-face community experiences. The Christian instinct to form community thus corresponds to a real need in society.

Not surprisingly, there is much in common between these two reflections on the signs of the time through which the Spirit is inviting the Church today to respond.

To conclude our reflection we can do no better than quote one of the most influential Christians of modern times, Dietrich Bonhoeffer, who courageously returned to Nazi Germany during the war to end up in prison in April 1943. Despite all appearances to the contrary, the resurrection of Jesus gave him hope as he wrote to his parents on Easter Sunday 1943:

> *At last the tenth day has come round and I am allowed to write to you again. I do want you to know that I am having a happy Easter in spite of everything. One of the great advantages of Good Friday and Easter Day is that they take us out of ourselves and make us think of other things, of life and of its meaning and its suffering and events. It gives us such a lot to hope for.*[38]

6

ECUMENISM TODAY[39]

TO AN OUTSIDER the relations between Christians over the last few hundred years would seem like the situation of the six blind men of Indostan, which we learned as children.

> *It was six men of Indostan*
> *To learning much inclined,*
> *Who went to see the elephant*
> *Though all of them were blind;*
> *That each by observation*
> *Might satisfy his mind.*

Each man, the fable runs, took hold of the elephant at a different place, and each concluded from his limited experience what sort of animal this wondrous elephant was. One bumped into its side, so he decided that the elephant was very like a wall. Another took hold of its tusk and therefore concluded that it was very like a spear. A third thought that the elephant was similar to a snake, because he had grabbed its squirming trunk. A fourth who clasped it by the knee thought it was very like a tree. Another felt its ear and thought it was like a fan, and the sixth blind man concluded that it was very like a rope.

> *And so the men of Indostan disputed loud and long.*
> *Each in his own opinion exceeding stiff and strong;*
> *Though each were partly in the right,*
> *And all were in the wrong.*

Christians in their disputes, their differences, their power struggles, seem blind to the central command of Christ: 'Love one another as I have loved you ... by this shall all men know that you are my disciples'.

This love should extend even to one's enemies. This love should bind the followers of Christ into a unity like the unity of Christ and the Father himself, and most important, this unity would lead the world to believe that Jesus came from the Father. Unfortunately, Christians, like the Jewish nation of old, which was called to be God's servant and a light to the world, became almost a counter sign. The result is that the world does not believe in Jesus and the Churches have so often become symbols of prejudice, mistrust, misunderstanding, bitterness, power struggle from Northern Ireland to South Africa. A recent writer said of Northern Ireland that there are many Protestants and many Catholics but too few Christians. It is a shocking thought that for centuries, the vast majority of Christians have lived with little or no practical concern for the fulfilment of Christ's prayer for unity, that is, apart from a few courageous pioneers who suffered for their prophetic opinions and were so often dismissed and rejected as imprudent and impractical.

That the picture in Africa was never a completely negative one can be seen from such outstanding examples as those mentioned by Adrian Hastings:

> It is good to remember that the Catholic proto-martyr of modern Africa, St Joseph Mukasa Balikuddembe was killed in 1885 because he had bravely spoken up against the murder of the Protestant Bishop Hannington; that the last night the body of David Livingstone spent in Africa was in a Catholic chapel of the Holy Ghost Fathers at Bagamoyo; that it was a Protestant minister who presided over the funeral and prayed at the grave of Bishop de Marion Bresillac in Freetown in 1859. Best of all our martyrs died together; Catholic and non-Catholic were burnt side by side at Namugongo for their common belief in Christ, the Protestant Alexander Kadoko as well as his uncle, the Catholic Bruno Serunkuma (Church and Mission in Modern Africa, Burns & Oates, London, 1967, p. 247).

The Ecumenical Movement:

The ecumenical movement, properly so called, dates especially from the time when Protestant missionary groups, transported from the situation of the home countries, began to realise that the divided Christianity which seemed so important at home was really ridiculous on the missions, and in fact a scandal and a hindrance to the preaching of the Gospel. Protestant Churches had been particularly affected by the separatist tendency. In the sixteenth century, there were four principal divisions, Lutheran and Reformed, Anglican and Free Church. But by the nineteenth century, the Lutherans, for example, had 81 distinct denominations in the United States alone. These in return were reduced to three principal bodies by 1970. It is difficult to pin-point the origin of the ecumenical movement. In fact over a period of 150 years in a variety of circumstances, forms, places, a longing to reach across the divisions and barriers, became increasingly evident. The World Missionary Conference in Edinburgh in 1910 which brought several Protestant missionary societies and churches together was an important foundation which blossomed into the World Council of Churches.

The Catholic Church was a late and hesitant arrival on the scene. The late English Cardinal Heenan used to tell this story about his childhood:

> When I was a small boy, we often had to fight our way to school. Protestants threw stones at us and shouted insults. We, to be sure, also threw stones, and no doubt, often threw the first stones.

The famous encyclical, *Mortalium Annos*, written by Pope Pius XI gives the typical official attitude of the Church which prevailed for many years:

> 'We are certain,' he wrote, 'that it (ecumenism) is an easy step towards negligence of religion, towards the indifferentism and modernism whose unfortunate adherents claim that dogmatic truth is not absolute but relative ...'

Ecumenism meant, at best, a return to and a complete submission to the Catholic Church.

Pope John XXIII and the Vatican Council:
Pope John and the Vatican Council marked a decisive

84

change in the Catholic approach. In particular, the warm and open personality of Pope John did much to allay the suspicions with which Catholics were viewed in Protestant circles. He made ecumenism and Church unity one of the principal aims of the Vatican Council. Nearly all Christian Churches were represented at the Council by observers, who exercised a real influence on the course of the Council.

A few quotations from the Vatican Council's Decree will show us how seriously the Council viewed the ecumenical movement.

> *The Sacred Council exhorts all the Catholic faithful to recognise the signs of the times and to take an active and intelligent part in the work of ecumenism (par. 4).*
> *Concern for restoring unity pertains to the whole Church, faithful and clergy alike. It extends to everyone, according to the potential of each, whether it be exercised in daily Christian living, or in theological and historical studies.*

Thus, it would be clear that ecumenism is not an optional extra for a Catholic or something to be left to the Bishops or to ecumeniacs or peripheral Catholics. Here the Council comes as near as in any of its recommendations to a direct law or command, calling *all* Catholics to play their part.

Perhaps the most unusual and important aspect of the Council's Decree is its remarkable admission of guilt and repentance for past failures. I quote:

> *St John has testified: 'If we say that we have not sinned, we make him a liar and his word is not in us' (1 Jn 1:10). This holds good for sins against unity. Thus in humble prayer, we beg pardon of God and of our separated brethren just as we forgive them that trespass against us' (par. 7).*

The Meaning of Ecumenism:
What does ecumenism mean for us if we are to be faithful to the Church's call? Perhaps it is better to begin by saying what ecumenism is not, as there are many vague ideas floating around, and many dangers into which a superficial and indiscriminate enthusiasm can easily lead.

Ecumenism – What it is Not:

1. Ecumenism does *not mean a return to the Roman Catholic Church.* To return means to have left the Roman Catholic Church. Obviously, we are not dealing with such people to-day. Even if we go back in history, we can perhaps best understand Luther as a reforming Catholic who had no de-sire to divide the Church.

2. Ecumenism does *not mean the watering down of truth* or a compromise based on the lowest common denominator. Pope Paul tells us *(Ecclesiam Suam):*

> *The desire to come together as brothers must not lead to a watering down or subtracting from the truth. Our dialogue (with our separated brethren) must not weaken our attachment to our Faith ... We cannot make vague compromises about the principles of faith and action ... Only the man who is completely faithful to the teaching of Christ can be an apostle; and only he who lives his Christian life to the full can remain uncontaminated by the errors with which he comes in contact.*

Thus, ecumenism, if it means anything, means complete fidelity to Christ, and no feeble half-measures; it means love; and if anything is weakened, it is suspicion, hatred, division, etc., not faith, not love.

3. Ecumenism does *not mean relativism or indifferentism* – the kind of thinking that says one Church is as another, or the kind of thinking which glosses over genuine differences and suggests that any point of view is equally valid, provid-ed it is sincerely held. Ecumenism not only means convic-tion, but also sympathy and respect for those who think and act differently from oneself.

4. Ecumenism does *not mean a desire for uniformity.* Perhaps the best schemes of union worked out so far,' writes John Macquarrie, Professors of Divinity at Oxford, 'have been those between the Roman Catholic Church and the Uniate Orthodox Churches. Here the various liturgies, customs (e.g., married clergy, etc.) and languages have been pre-served in their integrity. I think it was Augustine who de-

scribed it well, as unity in essentials, freedom in doubtful matters, but charity in everything. The Churches have begun to recognise in recent years the importance of legitimate variety, and the enriching and creative possibilities of pluralism in the Church, in liturgy, etc.

Ecumenism – What is it?

1. Ecumenism is an entering into dialogue with other Christians to try to discover what Christ wants for us all. It is a common search for, and looking forward to the visible unity of the Christian Churches, which express that which already exists due to our common baptism into Christ.

2. It is an attitude of mind characterised by a humble admission of personal guilt and responsibility, an absence of triumphalism and self-righteousness and a realisation and acknowledgement of not having all the answers, it is an attitude opposed to Pharisaism and basic un-christian attitudes.

3. 'There can be no ecumenism worthy of the name,' the Vatican Council tells us, 'without a change of heart. For it is from newness of attitude (*cf.* Eph. 4:23), from self-denial and unstinted love that yearnings for unity take their rise and grow towards maturity.'

It means basically a conversion to Christ, a becoming more Christian for each, a coming closer to Christ and therefore a finding of each other in Christ. It means the kind of renewal for the Church that the Second Vatican Council called for, an acceptance of the Second Vatican Council's key principle that *ecclesia semper reformanda* – the Church is in continual need of renewal, of reformation.

4. Ecumenism means avoiding the old controversial and polemical ways of dealing with our separated brethren,

> *every effort to avoid expressions, judgements, and actions which do not represent the condition of our separated brethren with truth and fairness (par. 4).*

Cardinal Willebrands, once President of the Secretariat for

Christian Unity, gives an excellent example of an honest re-appraisal of Martin Luther:

> 'Martin Luther,' he writes, 'has not always been correctly appreciated by the Catholic side in the course of centuries, and his theology has not always been correctly presented. This has served neither truth nor love, and therefore it has not served the unity we are trying to establish. Who could deny that Martin Luther was a profoundly religious person who sought honestly and with self-denial, the message of the Gospels? Who could deny that in spite of the torments he inflicted on the Catholic Church, he preserved a substantial sum of the riches of the ancient Catholic Faith? Luther in an extraordinary manner for his time made the Bible the starting point of Christian life and theology. Did not Vatican II meet demands which among others had been voiced by Luther and through which many aspects of Christian faith and life can find better expression than before?'

5. Ecumenism means meeting together in a spirit of true Christian dialogue. It means that we need each other; that we are incomplete as long as division continues. Dialogue means an anxiety to listen to one another, an interest in the teaching, the liturgy and the experience of our separated brethren and the opinions which they have of us and vice versa. Dialogue is based on the 75% we have in common – for too long we only saw the 25% on which we thought we disagreed. Yet, if you really consider the question, we have 99% in common, i.e., what is most important, Christ. What else is there to add to our common faith in and acceptance of Jesus as our Lord and Saviour, our common Bible, our respect for one another's good will and religious freedom, etc. As we get to know and trust each other better, we can face and examine the percentage which seems to divide us. Surely we will be able to surprise ourselves, and produce as they did in the Anglican/Catholic dialogue, agreed statements on the Eucharist, on Ministry and Ordination.

6. One of the best ways of drawing the Churches together is practical co-operation and collaboration which we so often see nowadays in face of the afflictions of our times, such as famine, world war, natural disasters, illiteracy and poverty, lack of housing, the unequal distribution of wealth.

This is a vital area on which we can all question ourselves. Ecumenism should not so much result in a mutual admiration society of Christians turned in upon themselves, as it should continue the work of Christ and turn all Christians out to the world where two-thirds are not receiving the vital minimum of calories daily; where 83% live under varying degrees of desperation and degradation, poverty, disease, economic and political oppression; where in fact, a large proportion of mankind have never really been confronted with the Gospel message. It is a sad thought that it takes a disaster and a catastrophe (e.g., Second World War) to bring Christians together. Is not Christ a sufficient motive?

7. Ecumenism means especially and above all prayer, and prayer together, to ask God to send his Spirit to unite Christians together, something which we cannot do ourselves. The story of Humpty Dumpty is an apt illustration:

> *Humpty Dumpty sat on a wall;*
> *Humpty Dumpty had a great fall;*
> *All the king's horses and all the king's men*
> *Couldn't put Humpty together again.*

Only the Spirit can move the mountains and put Christians together again.

We have come a long way in recent years and witnessed tremendous achievements in Christian co-operation in education, medicine, social development programmes, Bible translation, student chaplaincies, religious broadcasting. In Kenya, for example, they have achieved a unique common syllabus for the Religious education of their children. We are not so ready to judge another Christian Church according to our own ideals, forgetting our sinful reality. We see Catholics recognising the values of variety and plurality, whereas Protestants recognise the need for greater unity. Catholics have placed more emphasis on the Bible, Protestants on Tradition. The list is endless. The situation has changed so rapidly that we are suffering from a kind of ecumenical shock. It is clear that we cannot return to the supposed good old days when our beliefs and antipathies were so clear cut yet often remote from the mind of Christ which urges us to break down the barriers which separate people today, whatever valid reasons there may have been for erecting them in the past. Yet a superficial lets-all-get-together now and forget the past approach is evidently too simple. The way of ecumenism is essentially the way of self-denial, the cross if it is Christian. Again indifference is an option to be avoided. No true Christian can be satisfied to say 'I'm saved' and ecumenism doesn't matter. We need to face the real situation where we are to ask such simple questions as What does Christ want? What can I do now?

Much has been achieved after the impasse of the centuries has been conquered, but much is still to be done. The danger is, that after the first enthusiasm, the ecumenical movement seems to have run out of steam. Even when we pray for 'Christian Unity' our attitude and hope is not unlike those who pray for a happy death, or like Augustine's prayer for chastity – something theoretically desirable, but not a matter of any great urgency and preferably far in the future.

The situation for the Christian is always urgent. Any refusal to commit oneself to promote actively genuine Christian Unity is a betrayal of Christ and the Church. Each of us has a unique contribution to make so that the world may believe! The question which we should bring with us as we leave this reflection is, What am I going to do?

7

DIALOGUE TODAY[40]

'DIALOGUE' IS ONE of those magical words which have become popular since the Second Vatican Council. But like so many of these 'in-words' it means different things to different people. Like 'fulfilment' some see it as a universal panacea for all the ills in the community, while others think it destructive of all that religious life seems to stand for. A modern wit has suggested that poverty, chastity and obedience have been replaced by availability, friendship and dialogue. However, it is obedience in particular which many think threatened in these post-Conciliar times.

Obedience and the Bible:
It may come as a shock to some to find that examples or instructions on religious obedience as such are difficult to find in the Bible. Recommendations to poverty and chastity are not hard to uncover in the gospels, but I cannot find a single New Testament text on which the evangelical counsel of obedience can be based directly. This is a serious fact, given that the Church propounds the Bible, and especially the gospels as the measure and keystone upon which a Christian life should be based.

There are in the Bible clear recommendations to obedience to the Apostles, to bishops and to civil authority. The Vatican Council in the *Decree on the Religious Life*, points to certain texts which show Jesus' obedience to his Father (Jn 4:34; 5:30; Heb. 10:7). In his public life Jesus constantly looked to his Father and did his Father's will, but not to any human superior apart from his parents and the public authorities of his time. Nor did he urge his disciples to place themselves under such obedience. The primacy of Peter does not seem to mean that the other disciples should obey him in all things, and still less requires a vow to do so. All Christians are expected to obey the Father's will and to pay tribute to Caesar, just as Christ did.

Although the actual word 'obedience' and its derivatives occur some 87 times in the New Testament it seems to have never been used by Jesus. Yet he made some extremely difficult demands on his followers. But obedience does not seem to have been a question of carrying out orders. Rather it involves a firm decision for God and his demands in the concrete situation. Further, it is evident for Jesus that the strict interpretation of the law and Jewish tradition does not always point to God's will in the particular situation.

Return to the Gospels:

There is little in the gospels to support the detail of religious life and obedience as it came into the twentieth century. Then a superior seemed to have a direct line to God and the subject was confident that his response to the liberating gospel of Jesus was to be found in obeying detailed rules and every wish of the superior. There can be no doubt that the Second Vatican Council invited religious to reform, to take as –

> *the fundamental norm of the religious life ... the following of Christ as proposed by the gospel*

and only secondly to return to the original inspiration of the founder. We know that a dispute took place over the order here, as to whether the gospel or the founder's inspiration should come first.

Love, says the gospel, is what a Christian's life is all about. We can see that the lately renewed constitutions of the various religious societies stress the *primacy of charity* and the fact that obedience, and dialogue too for that matter, must be understood *within the context of Christian love*

(Agape). It must be the result of the working-out of love. For apart from love, it is a 'noisy gong or a clanging cymbal' (1 Cor. 13:1). This may seem to be stressing the obvious, but where love ('patient, kind ... always hoping ...') rules a community it is difficult to see many of the familiar problems of obedience and dialogue occurring when both authority and obedience are informed by this kind of spirit. No thinking person denies the necessity of some kind of authority and obedience in any society. Otherwise life would be unthinkable and unliveable, and traffic conditions for example would be suicidal. For the Christian it is important to know what kind of authority and obedience Christ himself wanted for his community.

Christ's Example:

A recent writer has suggested that there was little dialogue between Christ and his disciples. After the first prophecy of the passion (Mt. 16:22), we remember how severely Peter was rebuked for his protest, so severely that after the second and third prophecies the disciples did not venture to ask for an explanation, even though they did not understand. Nevertheless, what we should examine and reflect on are the actual examples which Christ gave to us to imitate the washing of the disciples' feet. Christ could say 'Moses said, but I say to you ...' and no superior can say that. We would call it 'playing at God'. No superior can read peoples' minds like Christ. His way of teaching certainly encouraged original thought, examination of the reasons behind rules and a hierarchical interpretation of them, rather than what we call blind obedience. This was a fulfilment of Jeremiah's description of the new covenant –

> *I will put my law within them and I will write it in their hearts and I will be their God and they shall be my people. And no longer shall each man teach his neighbours and each his brother, saying 'Know the Lord' for they shall all know me from the least of them to the greatest ...*

Much of Christ's teaching was Socratic, in the form of questions addressed to ordinary people, as at Matthew 21:28, where he begins –

'What do you think? A man had two sons ...' or earlier at Matthew 16:15, 'But who do you say that I am?'

Scholars stress the unique nature of this kind of teaching. There is no parallel in rabbinical literature.

The Second Vatican Council:
In modern texts it is interesting to note the emphasis on the obedience of the superior. For the superior, too, has a vow of obedience and the office provides no dispensation. Authority is but a form of obedience, an exercise of love of God and one's neighbour. The treatment by the Vatican Council of this point is interesting. When speaking of the obedience of subjects its words are traditional. But when speaking of superiors it insists, for example, on 'consultation' and 'giving a hearing'. This reflects some of the strong statements made at the Council. One Superior General said quite bluntly that the talk heard so often about a crisis of obedience should be called more properly a crisis of authority, of superiors. Superiors, he said, do not know when or how to call a meeting or to consult the needs and wishes of the community. It is interesting to see that the word 'dialogue' is conspicuously absent from the *Decree on Religious Life*. This led me to an examination of the development of the notion of the word in the documents of the Second Vatican Council using a detailed index.

In 1963 the first documents on the *Sacred Liturgy* and *The Instrument of Social Communication* were produced. The notion of dialogue is quite absent.

In 1964 the *Dogmatic Constitution on the Church* and the *Decree on Ecumenism* and *Eastern Catholic Churches* were brought out. The notion of dialogue is clearly present in only one of the three, the *Decree on Ecumenism*, in which it is mentioned approximately sixteen times.

In 1965 three sets of documents were produced:

a) 28 October: Five Documents on *The Bishops' Pastoral Office in the Church, The Appropriate Renewal of the Religious Life, Christian Education, Priestly Formation* and the *Relationship of the Church to Non-Christian Religions*. An average of four references to dialogue can be found in each with the exception of the *Decree on Religious Life* in which no reference is found.

b) 18 November: *The Dogmatic Constitution on Divine Revelation* has no entries in the index, while the *Decree on the Apostolate of the Laity* has five.

c) 7 December: The final four Documents were produced. There is one entry for the *Declaration on Religious Freedom*, six for the *Decree on the Church's Missionary Activity*, two for the *Decree on the Ministry* and *Life of Priests* and thirty-five for the *Pastoral Constitution on the Church in the Modern World*.

There is then a clear development in the use of the notion of dialogue between the first documents of the Council in 1963 and the final ones produced two years later. One can also see a development from the Council's *Decree on Religious Life* to more recently produced official documents and renewed constitutions.

Modern Emphasis on Dialogue:

The function of dialogue has been emphasised (or rediscovered perhaps) in modern society as a basic element in all human relationships especially between those in authority and the members of their communities. The Vatican Council applied the notion in five main areas of our human relationships:

a) Dialogue between a person and God (*Gaudium et Spes*, par. 19).

b) Dialogue between those who think differently, have different cultures, between classes and nations (*Gaudium et Spes*, pars 28,56). The *Declaration on Religious Freedom* tells us that:

Truth ... is to be sought after in a manner proper to the dignity of the human person and his social nature. *The inquiry is to be free, carried on with the aid of teaching or instruction, communication, and dialogue. In the course of these, men explain to one another the truth they have discovered, in order thus to assist one another in the quest for truth. Moreover, as the truth is discovered, it is by a personal assent that men are to adhere to it* (par. 3).

Young people, we are told in *The Declaration of Christian Education* should be trained to:

take part in social life ... be ready for dialogue with others (par. 1), while dialogue between old and young is to be encouraged (*Decree on the Apostolate to the Laity*, par. 12).

c) Dialogue between the Church and the World, the whole human family, between believers and non-believers, between Christian and non-Christian nations (e.g., *Christian Education*, par. 8, *Laity*, par. 14, *Church in the Modern World*, par. 21, *Missionary Activity*, par. 38). The basis for this dialogue is 'the dignity of the human person' (*Modern World*, par. 40).

d) Dialogue between Christians. See especially the *Decree on Ecumenism* (and *Modern World*, par. 92).

e) Dialogue within the Church, between priests and people (*Priestly Formation*, par. 15, *Laity*, par. 25), and between a bishop and his priests and people (*Bishops' Pastoral Office*, par. 13,28).

What is Dialogue:

This is the important question and like so many notions it is easier to say what dialogue is not than to tell what it is. Dialogue is not silence, but a risk, a willingness to take the initiative even at the cost of rejection from one's own community – which is the hardest rejection of all. Yet God could do the same. Dialogue is an attempt at bridge-building, at communion (the root *mu* meant 'to bind together'). For a Christian,

Christ is the basis and the Eucharist the ideal – no more male or female, Jew or Gentile, slave or freedman. All are one together because they are one with Christ. This has to be worked at throughout life – 'Work at love' is how Paul puts it.

Dialogue is not monologue, but an acceptance of the other person, on the basis of 'the dignity of the human person', where the person is at and not where we would like him or want him to be. Dialogue is listening, not selectively – hearing what we want to hear – but to the whole of what is being said. The song *Sounds of Silence* reminds us of those who 'talk without speaking, who hear without listening' and a recently popular poster challenged:

> *I know you believe you understand what you think I said but I am not sure you realise that what you heard is not what I meant.*

Dialogue is not small-talk or chatter. This is a world full of loneliness. The Beatles sang of 'all the lonely people'. People are now almost pathetic in their eagerness to talk, to speak the truth about serious problems and real issues, in their desire to be taken seriously, in accepting people for what they are, as important to God and to each other.

Dialogue is not controversy or confrontation. It is a common searching for Christ and for his relevance today. It means that neither knows everything or has all the answers. It recognises the need for one another and that there is a possibility of learning from one another. It is a common search. 'Seek the Lord and live' is to some of the ancients the key commandment of the Old Testament.

Dialogue is not domination by either side, but service. 'I may be your servant,' says the old phrase 'but you are not my master'. For the Biblical view is that the Christian lives and finds happiness through suffering service to God and our neighbour. The key words in the Bible include 'servant', 'slave' and 'service'. They suggest a total dedication to God and describe regularly the great men in the Bible from Moses and Joshua to Jeremiah and Paul. Service to God is through service to others, to the community. This includes the service of correction, an aspect which is often forgotten in modern times. 'Admonish the idlers' says Paul in his first Letter to the Thessalonians, 'encourage the faint-hearted, help the weak, be patient with them all' (Thess. 5:14; see also Mt. 18:15–17 and Titus 3:10). Anyone in authority who does not challenge the standards of others with the gospel because he is afraid to lose popularity is making a travesty of Christian authority. Anything goes today and it is almost impossible to be a heretic. Yet the Christian gospel is a challenge which can be met through dialogue, when that dialogue ensures that the gospel's uncomfortable aspects are not left ignored.

Dialogue is not aimless, but about Christ and his message and the application of that message to our lives. It is not a watering-down of the message but a facing-up to the Cross which is essential to the Christian life. It can easily become a means of running away, but it must be decisive, not meandering. It forces us to take up our crosses. In this, dialogue is ongoing, a continual challenge. It does not mean becoming a fuller Christian in an instant but a gradual becoming, involving respect of the other person's gradual development.

Finally, dialogue is hope, that forgotten Christian virtue. Paul tells us that charity always hopes and so we cannot write off other people or categorise them. Hope is not based on any evidence of goodness or badness but on God's grace and power. All is possible to him who hopes. It is a faith which can move mountains.

In conclusion, we can say that dialogue is nothing new to a Christian but simply a new way of expressing the old virtues of faith, hope and charity. Thornton Wilder suggested some years ago that religions die out when their great words wear out. Certainly many of the great Christian words have been dehumanised and devitalised in our time. Charity which should express the joyous response of the Christian to the Good News means little more than tossing a coin to a beggar.

Love is what we see on the screen between film actors. Service means a joyless menial drudgery. Faith is believing what is absurd and what you secretly think is wrong. Hope is a vague feeling in a desperate situation that something might possibly happen. Words like eminence and superior have come to possess meanings which are unchristian, to say the least. We need to watch our words and to change them when necessary. Dialogue, I suggest is one of the better new ones which try to capture what the old words have lost.

8

THE CHURCH OF THE FUTURE[1]

FUTUROLOGY IS CERTAINLY not an exact science, particularly for a Church which believes in a mysterious Father-God who works through the crucifixion of his beloved Son. The Church too is intimately involved with a world which is changing at an accelerating speed. The pace is so fast that in many areas our human comprehension of what is really happening and how rapid change affects our lives, inevitably falters. A recent *Pro Mundi Vita* Bulletin (100) in describing the shock of the future, suggests that due to the explosion of science and technology which has characterised the end of the second millennium, we are witnessing a fundamental mutation. This influences our lives and very being not to mention the exercise of our most fundamental rights and obligations. In all probability our present-day world differs more from the world of the beginning of the nineteenth century than that world differed from the Neolithic world.

The end of a century, and what a century, but even more the end of a millennium inevitably brings anxiety, weariness and doubts with it, opening the way to all kinds of fantasies including a large share of gloomy prognosticators croaking their Aristophanic choruses, ranging from despair to apocalyptic visions of the future. There is at base the simple fear not only of the unknown but also of the all-too-well-known. In the west, in particular, Europessimism has become a fashionable and even dominant attitude whereby Europeans tend to despair that the world will ever fundamentally improve. Thus, to quote the popular French expression, Europeans have 'settled into the crisis' of Eurosclerosis. This pessimism has become part of the European experience produced by centuries of wars, revolutions and financial crises.

Perhaps many of us have not sufficiently realised what an amount of change has really taken place in the last twenty or thirty years. In the west, the demonstration slogans have changed from the 1960s revolution to ecology in the 1970s to the nuclear threat in the 1980s. Decolonisation has taken place and now two-thirds of UNO are formed by new, young nations. In the Catholic Church the centre of gravity is moving from the west to the south.

By the year 2000 over 70% of all Catholics will be living in the south, the direct opposite to the position at the beginning of this century. Against this background the enthusiasm generated by the Second Vatican Council has come up not only against the forces of reaction but also the human mess, not to mention original sin.

Buhlmann insists that slamming on the brakes is no way for the post-Vatican Church to get moving. He quotes with approval M. Singleton's study of the Church in West Africa which has for its title Moses' words to the Pharaoh, *Let my People Go* ...

> The priests want to go ahead but the bishops will not allow it. The seminarians want to go ahead but the staff will not allow it. The women want to go ahead but the men will not allow it. The young want to go ahead but the old will not allow it. The Nigerians want to go ahead but the expatriates will not allow it. The Protestants want to go ahead but the Catholics will not allow it. All of whom met in the course of this enquiry want to go ahead but power groups will not allow it.

For Rahner the future is always a source of surprises and the Church is the community of those who in reflective understanding await the unplannable as their salvation. Watching and waiting for this unaccountable future is a fundamental duty of the Church. The very survival of the Church in a meaningful way in many countries is what is at stake.

Clearly it is important to care about the future while

avoiding that anxiety which Jesus forbade in that beautiful passage in the Sermon on the Mount (Mt. 6:25–34). The key phrase 'do not be anxious' which is repeated four times could be translated 'do not be divided in soul' suggesting that one should give total and undivided trustful service to God. The common misunderstanding of these verses can be traced to the early seventeenth century idiom, 'take no thought', used in the King James translation. Jesus is certainly not advocating passivity or fatalism in the face of the evils of a changing world. He does insist on careful fore-thought and praises both those who hunger and thirst for justice and those who bear fruit and make peace.

Buhlmann (p. 184) quotes Conleth Overman's study of three possible scenarios for the future of the United States: the ideal future, the plausible future and the likely future. The ideal future, to which specialists give a 30% probability, is utopian. There, creative imagination finds alternatives. All are in the service of others and the Charter of Human Rights has become a reality. The plausible future, which is given a 50–50 chance of success, is constructed and manipulated by experts who have a solution for everything from the world economic crisis to ecology and the arms race. The third rather sorry outlook which can easily be applied to the Church has a 70% probability. This means that everything will go on as before with a strong emphasis on consumerism, looking more to quantity than to quality, living from day to day and inspired more by a backward-looking than a forward-looking attitude. Buhlmann's aim is to help us change, to see anew, to feel anew, think anew, will anew. He believes that it is within us to change the probability figures so that even a utopian future could become a reality. Even a glance at recent Church history shows that much has become a reality which was considered utopian or undesirable. If by the year 2000 the rearguard of the Church could arrive at the point where the vanguard is today ...

Granted that reality is always presenting us with fresh

surprises what can we say about the Church of the next decade from the basis of present tendencies and the signs of the times?

Walbert Buhlmann is like one of those Old Testament prophets who has the courage to analyse his world situation and invite us to ask ourselves basic questions. What can we do to serve and further God's plans? How must the Church of the future to a certain extent appear when it starts out on the third millennium of its history? Perhaps it is no harm to remind ourselves of the importance of such prophetic interpretations. The ancient Israelites should have disappeared in the melting pot of the empires of the Middle East like their neighbours Ammon, Edom, Moab and Philistines who left only traces which archaeologists would investigate more than two thousand years later. Few nations in history were so completely reduced, so frequently defeated in war, deported to far-off countries, reduced to a pitiful remnant, subjugated for so long to such a variety of foreign oppressors and nevertheless they survived! Why? Why were they able to survive, continually re-build their community, re-interpret and hand on a developing tradition which could give meaning, hope and direction to the subsequent generations? An important part of the answer is that the prophetic figures who were generally failures in their own lifetimes were able to work out a theological interpretation of history and of disaster and failure in particular. Their disciples succeeded in persuading a sufficient number of people to accept their interpretation and direction of history.

The prophets gave a timely warning against absolutising the traditional institutions of Hebrew life, including leadership, cult and even land. Commitment to Yahweh of the Exodus alone was vital. By stripping away all false assurances of security they provided hope for a repentant people. Yahweh, they insisted, could act in new and unprecedented ways but always in keeping with his covenant character of pure grace – even though Israel had broken her part of the covenant.

Isaiah and Micah gave marvellous descriptions of a spirit-filled, just king, a new Zion and a peaceful kingdom. Ezechiel unforgettably portrayed the dead bones of Israel coming to new life. Jeremiah and Ezechiel, conscious of the widespread corruption of humanity, proclaimed a new kind of covenant. Jesus was a surprising fulfilment of these hopes of Israel in a way no one quite expected.

From Western Church to World Church:
With the promulgation of the new Canon Law can one say that the impetus of the Second Vatican Council has come to an end with a period of consolidation, of order and discipline within and decisiveness and uniformity without, particularly with regard to 'enemies'? On the contrary, with the Second Vatican Council has the Catholic Church just begun to enter a truly new era as it moves from a European Church to a World Church? It seems evident that the latter will set the main agenda for Catholicism in the decades to come, 'the Church on the way to the year 2000' to quote John Paul II's phrase repeated four times in *Redemptor Hominis.* The first millennium was that of the Eastern Church, the second that of the western Church and now with the irruption of the southern Church we are witnessing the de-Europeanisation of Catholicism and the emergence of the world Church. While the Second Vatican Council and the first three synods which followed it were dominated by the western Church and its concerns, at the 1974 Synod the concern shifted to the Third World. Its bishops and theologians raised the burning issues which resulted in the key encyclical *Evangelii Nuntiandi.*

Today the Church and its mission are found in six continents, Europe, Africa, Asia, Australia, North and Latin America. Now we speak of mission in six continents because the not-yet Christians and the no-longer Christians are found today in all six continents. For example, in Germany, Church attendance among young Catholics from 1963 to 1973 fell from 52% to 19%; in Catholic Vienna Church attendance was down to 10%; in the suburbs of French cities 5% to 3%; while in the United States there were 80 million unchurched. Until the abrogation of the *jus communionis* by an instruction of Propaganda Fide in 1969, one could speak of missions or juridical territories or objects of missionary activity entrusted to missionary institutes. With the new instruction they have become local Churches with their own responsibility for evangelisation in their area. It is no longer a case of here the Church and there the mission to whom missionary aid is given. Rather the situation is one of mutual inter-church service in which all Churches have something to offer and all have room and scope to become missionary. Yet while the hell syndrome may have come to an end, no one can say that the missionary age is at an end. The simple fact is that by the year 2000 there will be a good 4,000 million non-Christians.

Latin America:

Latin America with 323 million Catholics in 1980 in contrast to Europe's 271 million forms part of the Third World with its most obvious problem of poverty. This is the tropical zone which encircles the globe. There, some 800 million human beings live below a minimum subsistence level and are subject to racial wars and natural catastrophes, exploitation of the poor by the ruling classes, unfavourable trade conditions with rich and powerful nations, caught between the two extremes of communism with freedom or capitalism without justice. Yet is was a once a rich blessed continent with a marvellous potential for the Christian invaders. Buhlmann asks:

> Who will there be to honestly rejoice when in 1992 the 500th celebration of the discovery of America is observed? Should we not speak rather of invasion than discovery? Already in 1762 Abbé Raynald was writing that it would have been best had America not been discovered. He calls the discovery a catastrophic event ... the then proud and happy inhabitants of the Americas who through the incursion of white Christians were robbed of their lands and lives. Will there be

proclaimed in 1992 as a sign of international reconciliation a great confession of guilt? Or will this sinister tale merely be 'filed away' with so many others?

Yet in the Church in Latin America a powerful process for change is under way. The silence of God for five centuries is mysterious. Now once again he seems to be summoning a Moses to free the oppressed people from servitude and poverty as the bishops and episcopal conferences raise prophetic voices, especially in countries like Brazil. The movement began with a few theologians and lay people in lectures and small groups. These came to realise that the firmly entrenched system could not be willed by God: a privileged minority upholding the status quo using all the power of the state to repress and exploit, a Church concerned only with the supernatural truths while teaching patience to the poor. Only the rich were to be seen at the divine services. A new radical line was taken which did not begin by enquiring into religious practices of people or abstract eternal truths but by analysing the concrete everyday situation, the hopes and joys, cares and sorrows of a people and asking how the God of life will want to free the people not only from personal sin and difficulties but also from socio-political injustices. No longer was there a hierarchical Church with a care of souls from above with priests appearing at an outpost twice a year, dispensing sacraments divorced from Church-related activities and not appearing again for another six months. The Latin American option for community and for justice as a part of integral salvation has already exercised a wide influence. At the 1971 Synod and in *Evangelii Nuntiandi* it was accepted that to work for justice, development, integral salvation was not pre-evangelisation or a means to an end but 'an essential part of evangelisation itself'.

What has all this to say to Europe? Buhlmann sees the once despised continent as a great sign of hope. The fact that such a hierarchical, sacramentalised, statistical Church could renew itself to such an extent in so short a time means that the European Church, despite its history of clericalism, should not lose heart in its expectations from its own grass-roots or react in fear as if the Second Vatican Councils definition of the Church as the people of God was a mistake. Further it should play its own part in eradicating the great guilt it bears towards Latin America. While the documents of Medellin and Puebla never expressly use the phrase 'liberation theology', they constantly insist that theology and pastoral care should be 'liberating' because every one of us in some way lives in a state of captivity.

Africa:

In Africa, poverty means unfavourable climatic conditions, unjust world trade conditions, being a football of international politics and their gruesome proxy wars, shortages of food, medicine and spare parts of all kinds, bureaucratic government, black markets, corruption and exploitation of the poor by the rich, a way of life which Julius Nyerere calls 'spiritual slumming'. Despite a favourable start with independence in the 1960s many African nations have failed to achieve lasting superstructures and face a rather bleak future. But above all the problem which continues to break out is that of African culture. Africa complains bitterly that its cultural identity was destroyed in colonial times and that Europeans did not respect it. From the discovery of new continents at the turn of the fifteenth century a prejudiced view of the rest of the world as devilish tended to dominate Europe. A common notion already set forth in Luther's *Commentary on Genesis* was that Africans descended from Ham and were under his curse. Seventy bishops at the First Vatican Council signed a petition for priests to be sent to Africa where 'the oldest of all curses afflicts those wretched Hamites' who are under the fearful empire of Satan.

From the 1950s Africa began to regain its cultural consciousness as well as to retrieve and become reconciled with its past. In his 1980 journey to Africa Pope John Paul II insisted that 'Africa has much more to offer the world community than its raw materials' and that it 'is called to mediate fresh ideals and insights to a world showing signs of weariness and narrow self-seeking'. What Africa suggests in particular is an intense reaction against the continuation of European domination in the Church, in which unity means a uniformity which includes theological textbooks, catechisms, liturgy, hymns, etc. With the Second Vatican Council there came a cautious mention of 'legitimate pluriformity' (*Lumen Gentium*, 13,24; *Sacrosanctum Concilium*, 37–40). The basic model is the radical precedent of Christ's incarnation (*Ad Gentes*, 10). Ten years later Paul VI insisted that the gospel must be translated not only into different languages but into different cultures, theology, liturgy, Church structures, so that the young who today have a great feel for their own culture should really understand (*Evangelii Nuntiandi*, 63). This is as much a problem in Europe as in Africa. There too the bishops are accused of lacking in courage and creativity. With the passing of Latin as a symbol of unity there is an almost panic fear of a break-up into sects. According to Barret's *World Christian Encyclopaedia* there are far more denominations and Churches than was believed, up to 20,800. The problem is to find a way between the obvious extremes. Our hope in particular is of an African renaissance. In 1980 its 59 million Catholics were 7.5% of the Catholic Church. By 2000 Black Africa will have a Christian majority of 57%.

Asia:

While Asia has the problem of poverty as in Latin America and the problems of culture as in Africa, what particularises Asia with 57% of the world's population, is that it is the most religious continent in the world and in particular the cradle of all the great religions. Yet it is only minimally Christianised despite some five hundred years of Christian missionaries. If one excludes the 40 million Catholics in the Philippines, only 1.73% are Christian – one million Catholics, seventeen million Protestants, five million Orthodox.

With hindsight, it is embarrassing to read the arrogance and sheer ignorance of the condemnation of Asian religions and cultures even from such saints as St Francis Xavier. Until Pope John XXIII, such expressions as heathens, infidels and devil worshippers could be heard in papal speeches. However, in recent decades a more sympathetic approach has tended to prevail. As scholars such as Pannikar have pointed out, love alone opens the way to the truth. Today there is widespread acceptance of the fact that the Holy Spirit is present and at work in Asian religions. Pope John Paul II emphasised this before representatives of Japanese religions in his 1981 visit to Japan.

> I find in the virtues of friendliness and kindness, courtesy and brav-
> ery so commended by your religious traditions, the fruit of that divine
> Spirit who in our faith is 'friend of humankind', who 'fills the earth',
> 'holds all together' (Wis. 1:6–7). Above all, this same Spirit effects in
> all persons and in all religions the opening to transcendence, the
> tireless seeking after God, that can only be the reverse side of God's
> seeking after humanity.

Just as we Catholics and Protestants today tend to emphasise what unites rather than divides us, can we Christians also seek common ground with Asian religions? Have we all the same God looking in love on all human beings, sending his Spirit and his differing prophets? What separates is the Christ of the creeds, the dogmas and the claims to unique-ness and exclusiveness. Obviously there is a lot which a Christian cannot omit if we are to remain Christian. But the emphasis on exclusiveness and uniqueness was so pro-nounced in the past that a note of 'Wait and see; we shall know in time' is an essential element in the way forward with other religions.

Christians, too long an exclusive club passing judgement on everybody else with little real knowledge of their reli-gions 'from within', need to journey again with a threefold

109

mission to the whole of humanity:

a) to interpret the world in terms of the all-embracing love of God, the good shepherd, to bring the good news of the gospel 'shalomising' the world by gifting it with peace and salvation;

b) to transform the world in deed and truth and not mere words, to aim at a more just and humane world;

c) to Christianise the world, to make committed credible Christians and not be content with a superficial baptism, a policy which was radically unsuccessful in Asia.

Justice, Peace, Hope, Fellowship:

Granted that different aspects of the message of Jesus have been emphasised in the course of the centuries, these four perspectives of the gospel, according to Buhlmann, are in the forefront of interest today. Under Justice he describes the more objective and self-critical attempt to write the history of the past which has prevailed in recent years and in which *audiatur et altera pars* (letting the other side of the question be heard). Yet historiography only reaches its fuller value when it provides an impetus to build community, an opportunity to shape and build the future.

For Buhlmann, in contrast to those who bemoan the present state of the Church, 'the Church, in what concerns her externals, is in a much better state than ever before since the first centuries. Not only has the way of peace been opened again with Jews, Protestants, non-Christians, non-believers, but the whole content of peace has been rediscovered afresh. The Church's sublime mission is one of *shalom* in the original and broad sense – personal fulfilment, blessing, wholeness, soundness, completeness both personal and communal, bodily health, psychological well-being, economic prosperity'. This new understanding was first developed in Latin America. The priority of the Church is not its own justification or extension but to serve humanity, to mediate integral salvation, to build a world peace community. For the Church to become a *koinonia* (community) of the one Church in all six continents, it needs an exchange on five different levels. The lowest, though of considerable importance, is monetary aid. The second rung is an exchange of personnel between all six continents. The third step is an exchange of theology in contrast to the western monopoly until the mid-1960s. Higher still is an exchange of pastoral experiences and experiments, especially in basic communities. The highest stage is an exchange of lifestyles, of models of faithful Christian life, of saints, of martyrs for justice.

Can one honestly say that there is hope for the western Church from the Third World, which, one must honestly admit, is itself in a hopeless state? Buhlmann is well aware, from his many travels, of people constantly bemoaning their own situation while being enthusiastic about another Church, another country, another missionary institute. Tanzania, once a sign of hope of a distinctively African socialism, has as much corruption, crime and economic ruin as elsewhere. There, Nyerere sought to create a model based neither on self-interest nor restricted freedom, a middle way between the extremes of capitalism and communism. At least it is a beautiful dream. But what is the alternative to a dream? Admittedly, 5% at most, of the people of Latin America is affected by the experiment in basic communities but so what! For Buhlmann

> the young Churches provide the older Churches with a good counter-balance to the over-earnestness of the western work ethic and efficiency. Many westerners have become robots, machine-tenders, and in so doing have forgotten how to be human beings, how to live in community, take part in family life, be glad to be alive, have faith in the future, respect old age. The young Third World peoples, with their spontaneous, warm-hearted ways, their hospitality, their joy in life in the midst of poverty, can heal the west of its insensitivity.

Already in the 1960s Jean Danielou foresaw that the worldwide Church would be helped to renew its liturgy from Africa and would benefit from the Asian sense of mysticism, meditation and spirituality. This prophetic view has already begun to be realised. For Buhlmann, in a world surfeited with words, theories, analyses, reports, addresses, books, the important thing is to take the step to praxis, to change reality. Francis of Assisi, loved and honoured not only by Catholics and Protestants but even by many of the unchurched, is his model. He did not reproach the Vatican, criticise the Church or condemn the feudal system of his Church and time; he simply acted in poverty, simplicity and love. We are fortunate to have such models in our time as John XXIII, Mahatma Gandhi in Asia, Albert Luthuli in Africa, Martin Luther King in North America and Archbishop Oscar Romero in Latin America.

In a novel by Anton Seipolt, the third century martyr Dionysius of Ephesus comes back to life and wanders through our post-Second Vatican Council period. He is surprised and disappointed by our Sunday sermons with their stress on morals and money, with little about Christ and no happy faces in the pews. He tells the archbishop that in his time preaching stressed what it meant to be baptised. After that commandments and prohibitions were no longer necessary. The archbishop honestly replied, 'We know we have to break new ground. But we are afraid'. Dionysius' constant message was 'Rejoice!' He saw the world as full of good people and the problem that they did not get along because they considered each other hopeless. The answer to Dionysius' message was 'Is that all?' When he fell asleep again the churchmen reflected, 'Sleep on, Dionysius, sleep more soundly this time! What did you wake up for?'

9

IS JESUS THE FUTURE?

PESSIMISM IS IN the air as we begin the last decade of this 'century of catastrophes', having just completed 'the greedy decade' of the 1980s – recent suggestions in *Time* magazine for a metaphor for our age include The Age of Mammon, of Global Uncertainty, of Inhumanity, of Instant Satisfaction, of Pre-Oblivion.

There are good reasons for pessimism. One has only to look at the world scene of Christianity today. Despite the final command of Christ to make disciples of all the nations the task seems hopeless even after two thousand years of missionary endeavours. In fact the percentage of non-Christians in the world seems to be growing and to be increasingly resistant to the Christian Churches – only 2 out of 7 are Christians.

Even among traditional Christians there is a considerable variety of vigour. A recent commentator, David Martin puts Sweden at one extreme, 'an established, unified, moribund and liberal church presides over a spiritual vacuum with just a tiny margin of fervid Pentecostalism and faith missions'. On the other extreme in America 'hundreds of competitive and dynamic denominations deal on a bullish market in souls'. Increasing secularism and liberalism seem to be corroding the vitality of strong missionary churches like Holland, Belgium, and even holy Ireland. Yet on the other hand, the Orthodox who incline more to the longer view, have returned to the Kremlin and Christmas is being celebrated officially for the first time in fifty years in Lithuania. One should mention also a growing sensitivity towards human rights, peace and justice and environment. Nevertheless John Bowden (*Jesus: The Unanswered Questions,* SCM London, 1988, p. 179) finds that the Christian tradition is disintegrating in a particularly complicated way because it is bound up with 'a part-religious, secular, technological attitude to the world which, as a result of western success in the commercial, military and paramilitary spheres and the global activity of the media, multinational corporations and international finance houses, is steadily spreading all over the world'. This secularised Christianity without Christ is a threat to any form of traditional religion and not least of all Christianity itself.

Walter Hollenweger in *Evangelism Today* (Christian Journals Ltd., Belfast, 1976, p. 29), reports a typical conversation about missions with his dentist.

> *'Stop talking about mission! Christianity has lost its cause. It could not stop two cruel world wars in our century. It is helpless before world-wide hunger. It cannot even convince the baptised Christians in Europe and North America of its truth. What is the purpose of offering the religion of the well-fed westerners to the hungry of the Third World? What they need are tractors, not tracts!' In these and similar words people have sometimes prophesied the end of mission to me. 'In the final analysis,' a dentist once said to me, 'it does not matter whether somebody is a Buddhist or a Christian. What counts is only the sincerity of his conviction.'*

Finally, Hollenweger reports that he found a chink in his dentist's armour by reminding him that one couldn't be a Buddhist and a dentist. For a Buddhist, the highest virtue is indifference, not only to one's own pain but to the pain of others. Thus, religion and theology do matter. One's theology or view of God, his involvement in the world and what he wants of us, do make an enormous difference in our world. Andrew Greeley insists that our view of God even determines which political party we vote for. The current slogan 'Don't just do something, stand there' is a reminder of our regular need to stand back, to calmly look at the realities in so far as we can dimly perceive the God of surprises at work.

Statistics and Megatrends: Although there is some truth in Benjamin Disraeli's adage that there are three kinds of lies, lies, damned lies and statistics, nevertheless, a statistical analysis and projection are an excellent aid. They provide a more objective view of the Christian World if one is to deal adequately with such statements as that before the year 2000, the Catholic Church will yield to Islam its place as the world religion with the largest number of adherents.

A very valuable statistical analysis is provided each year by David Barrett in *The International Bulletin of Missionary Research*. For 1989 he gives a total Christian population of 1.7 billion, with 908 million Muslims and 944 million Catholics – his projections for the year 2000 are 2.1 billion Christians, 1.2 billion Muslims and 1.1 billion Catholics. Christians were 34.4% of the world population in 1900, 32.80% in 1980, 33.1% in 1989 and 34% projected for the year 2000. The average number of Christian martyrs in 1900 was 35,600, in 1980 it was 270,000, in 1989 324,800 and for the year 2000 it should approach a half million. The number of foreign missionaries has steadily increased, 1900 (62,000), 1980 (249,000), 1989 (273,000) and 2000 (400,000). The unevangelised percentage of the world has steadily dropped from 48.7% in 1900, to 31.6% in 1980, to 24.5% in 1989, to 16.6% in 2000. The number of unreached peoples has dropped from 3,500 in 1900, to 1,200 in 1970, 700 in 1980, 475 in 1989 and 200 in 2000.

What are interesting are the four significant megatrends which have arisen since 1980. Firstly there is the rise since 1989 of the East Asian Colossus of 80 million Christians mostly Chinese, Koreans, and Japanese – 80% are charismatic and their missionaries are spreading across the globe. Secondly charismatics have spread throughout the 156 major ecclesiastical families – thousands of Christian institutions, hospitals, churches, schools, colleges, universities, publishing houses, broadcasting studios now have charismatic leadership. Thirdly there is the alarming rash of negative Christian activities since 1980. This includes, a rise in ecclesiastical crimes such as embezzlement ($300,000 in 1900, $30 million in 1980, $762 million in 1989, $2 billion in 2000), internal squabbles (500 schismatic denominations with 30 million followers have broken with Rome since 1900) and an escalating pre-occupation of western Christianity with its own welfare (99% of the total income of the Christian World is spent on itself). Barrett's fourth megatrend is the increasing use of computers, some 45 million with 200 million Christian computer specialists.

Theological Change since the Second Vatican Council:
Looking back on the Second Vatican Council which promulgated the 6 chapters and 42 articles of its *Decree on the Church's Missionary Activity* on 7 December 1965 (2,394 voted for and 5 against) it seems quite clear that the consensus was deceptive. The vital work was done with the indecent haste which marked the entire final fourth session of the council (*cf.* Fr. Gianni Colzani in *Omnis Terra*, September–October 1989, pp. 453ff). A seriously inadequate scheme of propositions had been withdrawn on 9 November 1964 (*cf. Doctrine and Life*, March 1983, p. 142) and the new document compiled by a small group of experts, was presented on 7 October, 1965. The discussion was far too brief because it comprised mainly of the sessions of the 8 and 11 October. Then the Commission declared the interventions complete and adequate on the 13 October. The result was a document which combined in rather uneasy harmony three of the many competing views of mission which were current; the classic judicial territorial concept of mission propounded in particular by the Propaganda Congregation; the thesis of the French *Parole et Mission* view which extended mission to the dechristianised societies of the west and the view of many North American bishops who agreed with Fulton Sheen's slogan that mission is wherever there is need.

Agreement? In the rush of so many ideas and publications

116

since the Second Vatican Council, can we say that any agreement has been reached? Professor Johannes Verkuyl of the Free University of Amsterdam whose *Contemporary Missiology* (Eerdmans, 1978) is widely used among Protestants as a textbook, insists that as we enter the last decade of this century, we must 'Confess that the task of world mission is unfinished' and that 'our common calling is to carry on with this task'. He suggests three items about which a consensus has been reached *(IBMR*, April 89, p. 55).

1) The goal of mission is the coming kingdom of God, and the communication of the gospel of the kingdom has four dimensions; proclamation, diakonia, fellowship and participation in the struggle against all kinds of injustices and for righteousness and peace. In simple terms the kingdom is God's gift but it is also our task.

2) The task should be fulfilled in co-operation among churches in all six continents. Communication of the gospel means a task *in, from* and *to* all six continents.

3) We need each other not only in theological developments but also in the proclamation of the gospel, in the diaconate, in the building of 'koinonia' and in the struggle against injustices and for righteousness and shalom (1 Cor. 12:12).

From a Catholic perspective the six decades of pilgrimage of the Swiss missiologist Walbert Buhlmann are typical. Drawing on David Barrett's statistics and Karl Rahner's theology, Buhlmann in his most important book, *The Coming of the Third Church* (English 1976) proposed the thesis that the centre of gravity of the Church was shifting from the western world to the southern hemisphere – by the year 2000 some 70% of Catholics and 60% of Christians would be living in the southern hemisphere. Buhlmann has progressed from an ecclesiocentric, exclusive and pessimistic view of salvation to a new vision which can be concretised in the following four points:

1) Beyond a Historical Eurocentrism: The Church for too long
has been identified with Europe and western culture. However, today Hilaire Belloc's famous comment that 'The
Church is Europe and Europe is the Church' is only a
memory of the past. We need to move away from all forms
of western superiority and monopolistic western expressions
in the Church. The famous address of Karl Rahner in April
1979 *(TS* 40, 1989, pp. 716–27) had highlighted the fundamental issue which lay behind the many concerns and disputes of that momentous council. Rahner concluded that it
was 'the Churches' first official self-actualisation as a *World*
church'. No longer can mission be seen in a one-way direction. The gospel can no longer be presented in a triumphal-
istic and paternalistic way as so frequently in the past. Since
the Second Vatican Council the expression of the Catholicity
of the Church has witnessed to an extraordinary variety of
contributions from the most unexpected places; from Asia
the importance of spirituality; from Africa a sense of community and celebration; from South America a concern for the
poor and a need to re-examine the structures of society; from
the United States a sense of the limits of theory or ideology
and the intractability of the real world, an emphasis on prag-
matism and the know-how of getting things done; from Europe the need for tradition, a sense of history and a respect for
ecology. In fact as Adrian Hastings *(African Catholicism,* p.
180) points out, the geographical vitality of popular Christianity has moved very rapidly in the second half of the century to become increasingly the religion of the non-European
dominated. The greatest achievement of the twentieth-cen-
tury church is its breakthrough to the non-white world.

2) Beyond an Individualistic Supernaturalism. Too often in the
past, the purpose of the Christian life was to save one's soul
from hell fire. Salvation was very individualistic, to accept
faith, to receive the sacraments to hope for eternal life. The
pendulum has now swung (perhaps too far) to this life, this

world, to the biblical 'now' and 'today'. There is much more emphasis on community and the quality of life. Salvation should be integral and embrace the whole person. According to Buhlmann, 'Revelation is for Revolution'. The paradigmatic Old Testament experience for liberation theologians was the Exodus where God came to Moses not just to give an inner religious experience but to redeem his people from slavery in Egypt, to lead them out so that they could become new people guided by his commandments.

> However Latin American theologians have developed their thinking to emphasise the New Testament insight of Jesus as 'Good news to the poor', and to examine the important contribution of a book like Job to an authentic spirituality.

3) Beyond a Narrow Exclusivism. Pope John XXIII had challenged the church to stress the positive, to say what we were for rather than what we were against, to dream again the gospel vision of goodness and service rather than privilege. So often the Church was against the spirit of the world, the signs of the times, against the Jews, pagans, Muslims, heretics. The Second Vatican Council put a great emphasis on dialogue with all people and an admission that the Holy Spirit is at work everywhere. The main task of the Church according to Buhlmann is not to be an ark of salvation for the privileged few inside but rather a sign of salvation for all giving a positive faith interpretation to our universe.

4) Beyond a Wrong Centralism. An exaggerated centralism is merely an expression of human power-seeking and structures. It sees uniformity as the guarantee of unity. Until the Second Vatican Council there was a strict uniformity in so many areas from liturgy to theology to morality and discipline, no matter what the culture. The Council began to speak of a legitimate pluralism and diversity and to emphasis the principle of incarnating Christ in each different culture. In *Antioch and Rome* R. E. Brown and John Meier showed the importance of a centre which holds. The Petrine office held the early Church together despite the extremes of the followers of James and Paul. Such a reconciling centre is required today more than ever, lest 'things fall apart'.

Is Jesus the Future for Mission?

To describe the constant change in our world of today, we need to update Heraclitus' old principle to 'You cannot step into the same river *once*'. Looking out with the faith eyes of a missionary, one is constantly surprised at the hopeful signs of the kingdom from the Kremlin to South Africa to South America. A recent issue of the *Economist* (4 March 1989) suggests that the light may even be shining at last in Africa. The editor begins by suggesting that Pliny's 'Out of Africa always something new' should, according to many today, be changed to 'something ghastly'. He lists the ghastly in detail: 'The real income of the average African is now 10% lower than in 1970. A baby born in Ghana is three times more likely to die before the age of four than one born in (poorer) Burma. AIDS has spread further in Africa than anywhere else: Half of all adult Ugandans may have it by the end of the century. The Sahara moves south, the Kalahari north, getting 100 miles closer each year. The Ivory Coast's rain forests have shrunk by four-fifths, its elephants all gone. Governments in Africa are changed by guns and 3 million refugees are living victims of fierce wars. In Africa it seems, life is still poor, nasty, brutish and short and likely to remain so'.

Despite this awful picture the *Economist* suggests that because of Africa's recent economic performance the light at last may be shining. Africa can take the main responsibility for its own development, if African leaders stop patronising their own people and blaming the rest of the world for many of their homemade economic woes, if outsiders stop patronising African leaders and talk to them as truthfully as to an American or a Frenchman.

The problem for the missionary is how to measure progress, granted, as Eugene Hillman (*Polygamy Reconsidered,* Orbis Books, 1975 pp. 65ff) well pointed out that progress in an area whether in wisdom, beauty, freedom, socio-economics, etc. should always be measured by retrogression in other areas of the same culture. For Hillman what is probably the only true universal norm of human progress is the concern, respect and love that people should have for each other. As is evidenced by the Good Samaritan pouring oil and wine into wounds, inadequate means might be combined with a high level of human sensitivity. Hillman quotes an anthropologist who claims that Eskimos and Australian aborigines, two of the so-called most primitive cultures are much more highly developed than the most so-called civilised cultures. They are very much more generous, loving and co-operative than are most of the members of civilised societies. They are honest, dependable, cheerful and courageous to a degree which comparatively few civilised people manage to become. Who then is more developed?

To say Jesus and his criterion of compassion are the answer proposes an answer which the west has never fully accepted. For His ideals are an indictment of much that goes under the notion of western freedom, progress and development if one takes the last century as an example. During this time western white people have been guilty of genocide, wholesale exploitation of subjected peoples, opium wars, the slave trade, the colour bar, apartheid, the production and use of weapons of mass destruction on civilian populations.

Jesus is the Answer. On reflection it will be a much humbler west which will find in Jesus the answer, not unlike the repentant Peter who asked 'To whom shall we go, you have the words of eternal life' (Jn 6:68)? The opening words of South African missionary Albert Nolan's *Jesus before Christianity* (Orbis 1980) are to say the least salutary:

Many millions throughout the ages have venerated the name of Jesus, but few have understood him and fewer still have tried to put into practice what he wanted to see done. His words have been twisted and turned to mean everything, anything and nothing. His name has been used and abused to justify crimes, to frighten children and to inspire men and women to heroic foolishness. The supreme irony is that some of the things he opposed most strongly in the world of his time were resurrected, preached and spread more widely throughout the world – in his name.

At the turn of the century the famous humanitarian Albert Schweitzer who dedicated most of his life to working in Africa wrote his provocative book *The Quest of the Historical Jesus.* Examining many of the nineteenth century lives of Jesus he showed that historical criticism is far from an infallible check on the vagaries of human imagination and has a capacity to produce a Christ in the image of its own ideals and prejudice. Many reflected the ideals and idiosyncratic practices of the Victorian writers themselves. The most famous of such lives by Reimarus and Strauss were 'written with hate' – 'not so much hate of the Person of Jesus as of the supernatural nimbus with which it was so easy to surround him'.

Today scholars insist that any credible portrait of Jesus must allow him to fit within the culture and problems of first century Palestine. While the available sources do not permit the reconstruction of a full biography of Jesus, that is in the modern sense of the term, nevertheless many recent scholars are convinced that a considerable amount of authentic material can be attained by using modern critical methods. These include the basic features and outline of Jesus' proclamation, behaviour and fate. Not surprisingly, the 1980 Melbourne Conference of the World Council of Churches *(Your Kingdom Come)* one of the best prepared and most important conferences on mission, saw a significant shift. As described by James A. Scherer in his excellent mission survey *Gospel, Church and Kingdom* (Augsburg, 1987, p. 142) the shift was from Paul and the apostles as paradigms for mission to Jesus Christ, healer, proclaimer and caster-out of demons as the missionary par excellence. It was a movement away from preaching a message of justification by faith to sinners, to enacting the kingdom in history by word and deed. Mission should be patterned on the ministry and teaching of the self-emptying of Jesus. Melbourne followed the lead of the two Catholic Conferences at Medellin (1968) and Puebla (1979) in declaring that the poor have a prior claim on God's promises and that the Church has a 'preferential option' to serve the poor.

Likewise, Don Senior in his valuable study *The Biblical Foundations for Mission* (SCM, London, 1983, p. 157) insists that Jesus and his mission are ultimately decisive for the character, the scope, the urgency and the authority of the Church's mission in every age. This centrality of Jesus to mission needs to be constantly emphasised judging by the provocative title *Missionaries Without Christ* given to an article in a recent issue of the Italian missionary journal *Mondo e Missione*. The author Professor Jesus Lopez-Gay points out that some writers even propose a Christianity without Christ as more relevant for today's world. The uniqueness of Jesus has in fact become the major issue in recent missiology. A recent conference on the question of religious pluralism has led to the volume edited by the Englishman John Hick and the American Paul Knitter entitled *The Myth of Christian Uniqueness* (Orbis Books, 1987). The shift in theology proposed by these writers has been described as the crossing of a theological Rubicon from an affirmation of the uniqueness of Christ and Christianity to a kind of parity of religions and a pluralistic view of religions as equally valid. Knitter who also published *No Other Name?* is quite unhappy with the traditional view of mission. He finds his stumbling block in the belief in the uniqueness of Christ which is central to Christianity. His view would open that possibility that Jesus Christ is one of many saviours and revealers in the world who are or can be equally valid. Such views of theological relativism have often been found in the past on the fringes of the Churches. What is new is that some of these voices are found in the World Council of Churches Programme as it prepared for its World Mission conference in San Antonio, Texas in May 1990. The editor of the *IBMR* bluntly comments that Christian missionaries cannot afford to cross such a Rubicon. Rather they need to affirm again the unique entering of the Creator into history some twenty centuries ago (Heb. 1:1–3). For without the uniqueness of Jesus' incarnation there is no gospel and certainly no mission.

Perhaps we can best leave the last words on mission to Mother Theresa. Criticised for her lack of success after so many years of dedicated service in Calcutta, she admitted the facts but insisted that the task of the Christian is not so much to be successful as to be faithful. One could quote also the words of the famous Maryknoll Bishop J. Walsh:

> *The task of a Missionary*
> *is to go to a place where*
> *he is not wanted,*
> *to sell a pearl whose value,*
> *although of great price,*
> *is not recognised.*
> *To people who are determined*
> *not to accept it*
> *even as a gift.*

NOTES

1 Prof. Palmaties, a linguistic professor at Western Michigan University in Kalamazoo, has just published a dictionary of some 1,700 sports metaphors which he says permeate every walk of life today. A.B. Biamatte (in *Take Time for Paradise: Americans and Their Games*, Summit Books, 1989) claims that 'we can learn more about the conditions, and values of a society by contemplating how it chooses to play, to use its free time, to take its leisure than by examining how it goes about its work'. He suggests that in sports 'some version of immortality is being sought whether by way of ritual or record and that under the rubric of leisure, sport – either watched or played – has availed itself of whatever prestige or privilege accrues to shared activities that have no purpose except fully to be themselves'. For Michael Novak (*The Joy of Sports*, Basic, New York, 1975, p. 48) the victories of sport are 'ritual triumphs of grace, agility, perfection and beauty over the process of aging and death'.

2 *cf* Thomas Ryan, *Wellness, Spirituality and Sports*, (Paulist Press, 1986, p. 136).

3 Philosophers have often been fascinated with games (see David Tracy, *Plurality and Ambiguity*, SCM, London, 1987, p. 17). Albert Camus insisted that he learned his ethics playing soccer as a boy in Algeria. For Ludwig Wittgenstein the category 'game' is central. Gadamer in his preface to *Truth and Method* used Rilke's famous poem which described how in some games we can be fortunate to begin to sense our resonance with the play of the cosmos itself. Edwin Goffman spoke of 'the games people play'. David Tracy speaks of the sense of freedom and ethical fairness peculiar to some games and the possibility of self understanding and freeing ourselves from ourselves however briefly through games. Both Plato and Aristotle defended the role of athletics in Greek paideia (*cf* Werner Jaeger, *Paideia*, Oxford University Press, 1945, pp. 205ff)

4 *Wellness: Your Invitation to Full Life*, Winston Press, 1981.

5 *New Catholic Encyclopedia*, p. 617.

6 1 Macc. 1:1ff; 2 Macc. 4:7ff.

7 Satires 10:77–18.

8 Beacon Press, Boston, 1950.

9 *Man at Play*, Herder & Herder, 1967.

10 *Summa Theologica*, 2a 2ae, 186.2.

11 *The Furrow*, December 1984, p. 757f.

12 Par 61; *cf. Christian Education*, par. 5.

13 31 December, 1939.

14 *New Catholic World*, July/August, 1986, pp. 182ff.

15 *Holistic Life Handbook*, And/Or Press, 1978, p 356.

16 T. Peters & N. Austin, Fontana, 1986, p. 181.

17 Is 2:1–4; Mic. 4:1–4.

18 Dn. 7:18.

19 Dn. 2:31–45.

20 Philip E. Berryman, 'Latin American Liberation Theology', *Theological Studies*, September 1973, pp. 359f.

21 Mt. 8:42ff; 9:39; 12:44ff; 28:30.

22 Jn 5:23; 8:42ff; 9:39; 12:44ff.

23 Is 8:14; Rom 9:23–33; 1 Pet. 2:8.

24 Num. 20:13; Dt 35:51.

25 Flannery (ed), *The Church in the Modern World*, par. 4, p. 904.

26 Abbott, *Documents*, p. 704, *Pacem in Terris*, April 1963, par. 126. In 1982, John Naisbitt, in his bestselling, *Megatrends: Ten New Directions Transforming Our Lives*, predicted that the United States would move from an Industrial Society to Information Society, from National Economy to World Economy, from centralisation to decentralisation, from representative to direct democracy, from Hierarchies to Networking or group efforts, from Either/Or attitude to Multiple-choice Option. If a politician can ignore these at his peril, what about Church leaders. He notes that all the tendencies, new ideas and initiative came from only five of the fifty states but then spread out nationwide. In his recent *Megatrends 2000* Naisbitt continues the same upbeat message. Americans need not be worried about the imbalance of trade, recession or unemployment as there are no limits to growth or supply. Rightly he questions the findings of the pessimists such as the Club of Rome forecasts of an overpopulated globe flooded with garbage and asphyxiated by fluorocarbons. In the *East Asian Pastoral Review 1989* one finds a very useful bibliography of the signs of the times.

27 (a) Flannery (ed), par 43, p. 15

(b) *ibid.*, 4, p. 456

(c) *ibid.*, 14, p. 798

(d) *ibid.*, 15, pp. 811–812

(e) *ibid.*, 4, 11, pp. 905–912.

28 Flannery (ed), par. 6, p 912.

29 14 September 1965.

30 *Teaching All Nations*, No 1, 1978, p .17f.

31 October 1974.

32 An interesting workshop on the Biblical Apostolate took place at Lusaka, Zambia, November 1978. It had representatives from 14 English-speaking and 2 French-speaking African countries. They analysed the aspirations, sufferings and development of their countries in terms of the great biblical themes of a New Creation, the Nazareth Manifesto of Liberation (Lk. 4:16ff) and the Magna Carta for an alternative society (Mt. 5–7). The concept of the three forces of interpretation originally developed by Carlos Mesters in Brazil was the guiding light of the workshop. These three forces of interpretation which identify the movement and quality of the Kingdom in today's society can be pictured as a triangle. Each is essential yet if considered alone threatens to distort the over-all vision of the new man, the new world proclaimed by the scriptures.

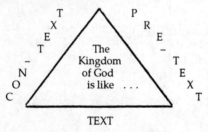

TEXT

The Biblical Text: This provides the inspired witness of past *ages* with regard to their encounter with God in the course of their own historical development. It gives definitive norms for what God wished to do for and with all mankind: an exodus-liberation from slavery (sin and all its consequences); unification of dispersed peoples while respecting the enriching pluralism of different cultures; reconciliation with God and with one another; the faithfulness of the divine commitment to man's full humanisation in community; and the prophetic vocation of this People of God to be a sign and an instrument of a new humanity. A reliable commentary is the normal tool to discover the original meaning of a particular text and what the vision and the demands of the Kingdom were for members of that particular community to which it was addressed. Whereas for some people today it is possible to begin from the Biblical text, for many others today the biblical experience is too distant a reality to make it easily a part of their own lives. For many (secular) people it is necessary to begin evangelising at that point where they are *most consciously suffering* (e.g., Christ's healing miracles). Some, it is necessary to bring to a 'consciousness' of their sickness which is often suppressed by a flight into formalism, consumerism and hyper-activity. This approach is to start with the 'signs of the times', both positive and negative which is referred to as the *Pre-text*.

Pre-text: This includes both positive and negative 'signs of the times' and involves investigating all that goes to make up contemporary, socio-political, historical milieu for indications of the presence and the absence of the Spirit already at work in society. The participants found that the legitimate aspirations, movements and events of the times are often too *ambiguous* to provide a clear summons to a faith commitment and are in need of clarification and identification. In fact they discovered that the negative signs of the absence of the Spirit were easiest to identify e.g., apartheid, alcoholism, injustice, exploitation, inequitable distribution of wealth, militarism, bribery, governmental corruption, promiscuity, prejudice, tribalism. They wrestled at length with the problem of formulating *criteria* for interpreting the contemporary signs of the *creative* activity of the Spirit, i.e., those great themes which permeate the totality of the Bible: unification, justice, equality, solidarity, liberation, etc. To accomplish this task today the same criteria should be applied to identify the Kingdom movements and the Kingdom qualities (See *Gaudium et Spes*, 38; *Evangelii Nuntiandi*, 20). This leads to the third element, the prophesying community – *Con-text*.

Con-text: The community of faith in prayerful dialogue with the definitive *norms* of the original inspired witness of the peoples of the Bible (Text) and in dialogue with the signs of the times discovered in the contemporary *Pre-text* forms the proper *Con-text* for a modern evangelisation of the world. Its task is to bring the other two elements together to become good news for the world today. Thus the heart of evangelisation they concluded is a dialogue of prayer, reflection on the signs and the searching of Scripture. In this very process they discovered a gradual transformation of their own attitudes and relationships whereby the actual participants themselves were becoming a true community. For a fuller report see Vol. 9/1/1979 of *World Event*, a publication of the World Catholic Federation for Biblical Apostolate, Stuttgart.

33 Max Warren, *I Believe in the Great Commission*, Hodder & Stoughton, London, 1976, p. 136ff.
34 Mt. 35:31–46.

35 Apoc. 21:26.

36 Rom. 8:26.

37 *The Tablet*, 5 November 1977, p. 1066. One could also mention the cumulative argument from the five signs of transcedence, which the sociologist, Peter L. Berger points to in a *Rumour of Angels*, significantly sub-titled 'Modern Society and the Rediscovery of the Supernatural', Allen Lane, The Penguin Press, 1971. From human experience, tragedy and evil, as well as joy and goodness, he argues for the recognition of a world beyond this. These are:

1) Man's trust in the order of reality without which he faces 'fundamental terror'. Is this propensity in man 'an invitation of ultimate reality'?

2) Man's joyful activity and play in which time stands still and he is drawn momentarily into 'beatific immunity'.

3) Man's hope, his 'No' to death which is profoundly rooted in his being and is seen in his 'death defying acts of courage and self-sacrifice'.

4) Man's utter revulsion at the presence of monstrous evil, e.g., concentration camps of which our condemnation is absolute and certain and not exhausted in terms of this world alone. This is the argument from condemnation.

5) The argument from humour. The comic reflects the imprisonment of the human spirit in the world, and humour, by laughing at this imprisonment, implies that it is not final.

38 Deitrich Bonhoeffer, *Letters and Papers from Prison*, Fontana Books, London, 1959, p. 143.

39 A lecture given to the Christian Churches in Nairobi during Ecumenical Week, January 1974.

40 From an address given to the Religious Superiors' Association of Kenya, April 1975 – published in *Supplement to Doctrine and Life* (Dominican Publications, Dublin, January–February, 1966, pp. 12–19).

41 A reflection on Walbert Buhlmann's *The Church of the Future*, Orbis/St Paul Publications, 1986, pp. xiii + 207, with an epilogue by Karl Rahner, SJ.